Teens Talk About
daTing

Ginny Williams

HARVEST HOUSE PUBLISHERS
Eugene, Oregon 97402

TEENS TALK ABOUT DATING

Copyright © 1994 by Harvest House Publishers
Eugene, Oregon 97402

Library of Congress Cataloging-in-Publication Data

Williams, Ginny, 1957–
    Teens talk about dating / Ginny Williams.
        p. cm.
    ISBN 1-56507-236-7
    1. Dating (Social customs)—United States—Juvenile literature. 2. Dating (Social customs)—Religious aspects—Christianity—Juvenile literature. 3. Interpersonal relations in adolescence—United States—Juvenile literature. I. Title.
HQ801.W715 1994
306.73—dc20   94-12472
                                                                              CIP

Printed in the United States of America.

94 95 96 97 98 99 00 — 10 9 8 7 6 5 4 3 2 1

*This book is dedicated
to all the incredible kids who form the
Youth Group of St. Giles Presbyterian Church,
Richmond, Virginia. Thanks for being my friends
and for teaching me so much!*

Acknowledgments

I joyfully acknowledge that this book is the result of the efforts of many people. I didn't really write this book, even though my name graces the front cover. It was written by the 72 young people who contributed questions about the things that concern them, and the 400 high school and college students who spent hours writing answers and sharing the lessons they have learned. I met a lot of incredible kids and made many new friends. Thank you!

My thanks also to Peggy Thorne and Rob Burns for making their kids available to me while I developed the questions; Edie Schulze for opening up the dorms of Wheaton College for me; Carole Trejos for putting up with my weird hours while she housed me at Wheaton; all the Resident Hall Advisers who rounded up the kids on their floors—Mary Thompson, Becky Norman, Jeannine Nyangira, Chris Walter, Kely Duggan, Matt Bubar, and Steve Offutt; Rick Dunn for letting me take over his Youth Ministry classes at Trinity College; Mollie Kleeberger for taking me to lunch; Wilma (Peach) Hoover for giving me all her students for two days, and for the privilege of speaking to her ninth-graders; Lara Harler for helping me round up students at Eastern College; Dee McCarter, Director of Resident Life at Eastern College; Duffy Robbins for leading me to the Lord and writing the Foreword for this book; LeAnn Blackert for letting me be her roommate for seven weeks while I worked on this book; Eileen Mason for believing in kids and their ability to speak to their own generation; Barb Sherrill for being an incredible editor and a good friend; and Harvest House for making this whole project possible.

Thank you!

Foreword

I'll never forget the afternoon Jim barged into my office at church. He was a good friend, one of the guys in my youth group, and somebody who would always shoot straight about his walk with the Lord.

But on this afternoon he was obviously pretty ticked off.

He threw himself on the scruffy old couch across from my desk and groaned, "Doggone it, Duff, I've had it. I've tried to keep myself sexually pure. I really want to be a godly guy. I'm really trying to do what the Lord wants me to do, but I've just had it. I try to have pure thoughts and everything, but I walk down the hallway at school and I see these great-looking girls in tight sweaters, and you wouldn't believe what goes through my mind."

Then he started yelling and pounding the arm of the couch.

"If God gave me these desires, why are they so bad? And if they are so bad, why did God give them to me? I know God gets disappointed with me, but I get disappointed too sometimes. I've had it. I'm just going to pray right now: God take away all of my sexual desire—"

I screamed, "Wait! Let me leave the room in case He misses!"

All of a sudden we were both laughing... and so far as I know, that prayer was never answered for either of us!

It seems like anytime adults talk to teenagers about sex, it's always in grim terms. I can still remember my junior high Sunday school teacher glaring at us and in a low, serious voice warning: "Sex is dirty, so save it for the one you love." This didn't make a lot of sense to me then, and it doesn't make much sense to me now.

Oh, I still think sex should be saved for marriage, but not because it's dirty. After 21 years of being married to an awesome woman who is also my very best friend, I think sex should be saved because it's too good to waste!

I guess that's what Paul meant in Romans 3:23 when He said that sin is falling short of God's plan. He didn't say sin was never fun, or that it wouldn't sometimes seem like a pretty good idea. He just said that it causes us to fall way short of what God intends us to have and to be.

God's plan is just like the law of gravity: You don't have to believe it or accept it, but there is a definite penalty for breaking it. And depending on where you jump from, you might do a lot worse than "fall short." Ultimately, sin leads to death.

But that's why I'm so excited about this book.

Ginny Williams has given us a book that doesn't try to tell us that sex is dirty. She helps us to see that it is a wonderful gift from God and that it's simply too good to waste.

In fact, what makes this book so different is that the author doesn't actually say much of anything. (No offense, Ginny!)

Instead, she lets people like *you* do the talking. She listens to *your* stories and let's *you* share from your own experiences. What makes these pages so unique is that most books are written by people who are good writers. This book is well-written by a person who is a good *listener.*

Ginny Williams cares about people like you. She's a youth leader with a warm heart, a fun spirit, an open ear, and...a word processor. And she loves Jesus. People like that can be dangerous! They impact lots of lives.

This book is like a really honest conversation between friends: you, Ginny Williams, the people who tell their stories in this book, and Jesus. Listen carefully to what you hear in these pages. You will hear these friends speak of memories too painful to visit, joys too wonderful to imagine, lessons too important to ignore, and a gift too good to waste.

Listen and hear, as *Teens Talk About Dating.*

Duffy Robbins
Chairman, Department of
    Youth Ministry
Eastern College, Pennsylvania

cOnTeNts

Why Teen Talk? 9

1. Am I Ready for This? 11

2. Finding Mr./Ms. Right 49

3. There's Nothing to Do
   Around Here! 83

4. Are We Really Supposed to Talk? 101

5. But I Can't Make Up My Mind! 111

6. The Parent Thing 125

7. Where Are the Brakes
   on This Thing? 143

8. Breaking Up Is Hard to Do 157

9. Is This It? 171

10. I Have This Problem... 181

Why Teen Talk?

Not long ago *Good Housekeeping* magazine and "CBS This Morning" conducted a telephone survey of 1013 teens on sexuality. One of the findings was that 89 percent said they paid more attention to their friends' views on sex and relationships than their parents' views.

The statistics were no surprise to me. Few teens go to adults first when they need help—not only about relationships and sexuality, but in most other areas of their lives. Although parents influence you, peer influence is more important. You go first to your friends because your friends are the first priority in your life.

And what about all the books written for you about dating, sex, alcohol, and suicide? Are they good books? Yes, they really are great. I read them and so do your parents and other adults. The problem is that *you* don't read them, so what good are they doing you? Especially if you're not talking to the adults who are reading them and getting all that great information to tell you. So there really is a problem.

Part of the problem is that some of the information you get from your friends is wrong! Let's say you're having a conflict, and you go to a friend who gives you some wrong advice. Now you have a worse problem. Example? You've been dating Scott for four months and you're really close. You think he wants to have sex, but you're not sure. You talk to a couple of your friends, and they say, "Hey, everyone's doing it! It's no big deal. If you love him, go ahead." Sounds like the kind of advice you wanted, right? So you go ahead. The next week Scott starts dating another girl, and you feel like a piece of dirt... and then you find out you're pregnant. Still think it was great advice? Hey, your friends thought they were helping. They didn't mean to mess up your life.

Now let's look at the flip side of this issue. A lot of your friends have really good answers for you. They've thought a lot about life. They're trying to live their lives the way they believe God wants them to. They've had some tough experiences that have taught them a lot. They know what it's like to live in your world and deal with the same pressures and stresses you do.

It's because there are plenty of kids like this that this book was written. The answers you'll find in this book come from the responses of hundreds of teenagers across the country (400 kids from 42 states, as a matter of fact). These kids have been where you are now and have asked the same kind of questions you do. They've come up with some pretty right-on answers that can help you. They've taken the time to write thoughtful and honest answers to hard questions. And they're willing to share their stories in order to help one of their own.

So I hope you enjoy the book. More than that, I hope you walk away with some answers to what's going on in your own world. God bless you!

chApTer 1

Am I Ready for This?

What is a good age to start dating? 13

How can I be friends with someone without
the person thinking I want to date him or her? 16

What if I want to be "more than friends"? 18

How can I erase memories
of bad relationships from my mind? 20

Is it better to have the security of a steady
relationship or the freedom of having a lot of friends? 23

Is it okay to date non-Christians? 25

Can I date someone
to try to bring him or her to the Lord? 30

Am I weird to not want to date? 32

Is it necessary to have a physical
relationship to have a good dating relationship? 34

When is the best time
to set physical limits in a relationship? 37

How do you know when
you're ready to kiss someone? 41

How can you know when you're
ready for a serious relationship? 43

How do you keep your relationship from making the
person you are dating first in your life instead of God? 45

What is a good age to start dating?

My parents made me wait till I was in high school to start dating. During my junior high years I was very upset at them for doing this to me. But now as I look back on it, after dating a lot in high school, I'm really glad I respected their rule so I could experience dating when I was more ready to handle it. I enjoyed not having to worry about dating during my junior high years. I just hung out with my friends and talked about girls.

Mike, 18

I think a good age to start dating is 16 or 17. I made the mistake of dating when I was 12 years old. The reason I say it was a mistake is because as I look back I realize I was really vulnerable to getting hurt physically and emotionally. I also think I didn't have much understanding about the opposite sex. Not only did I not understand them, but I didn't know what to look for in a relationship. It wasn't until my junior year in high school that I realized a relationship is built on a true friendship and not on superficial things.

Janie, 19

It isn't age; it's mental. When you decide that the measure of your worth is not in who, or if, you are dating, and you feel good about yourself the way you are, then you're probably ready.

Allison, 18

When are you old enough to date? When you're old enough not to. Often people feel they *need* to date. Or in some way they are pressured into it. If you feel you *need* to date for security, or companionship, or acceptance, then you're probably too young to date. Or at least there are still some things for you to learn. Relating to the opposite sex on a friendship level is challenging. Dating raises the stakes and muddies the water. Suddenly, once you've started to date, emotions begin to surface that you may not have known were there. How can anyone handle *that* if they can't relate to the opposite sex on a friendship level alone?

My question for anyone who wants to start to date, or who is already dating, is: "Do you grasp the significance of what you're getting yourself into?"

Robbie, 19

My dad would say (and sometimes I would agree) that 35 is a good age to start dating! To be honest, though, I think there might not be an actual age to begin dating. When you're old enough to be yourself and to not let anyone change you into who they think you could or should be, then you're old enough to date. Of course, it always helps to listen to Dad, too.

Rachel, 17

22—no, I'm just kidding. I was allowed to date when I was 16. Looking back over the last couple of years, I still feel like I knew nothing about relationships, dating, or guys. There are some key things: 1) Always build friendships with guys before dating. It's better for the relationship. 2) Don't follow everyone else. If you don't feel ready, or don't want to, don't let anyone persuade you that you should be dating. 3) Never be scared of dating because you feel like you don't know anything. You can learn through experiences, both good and bad.

Susan, 19

I used to think something was wrong with me if I wasn't dating by age 12 or 13. I thought I was the only girl in my freshman class who had never been on a date. But I wasn't alone. If you're in that boat, you're not alone. And you're really okay. The time to start dating is when you and God have talked about it, and you know that your self-image is not dependent on whether or not you have a date.

There is nothing wrong with waiting before seriously dating. In my case I brought each guy I was interested in before the Lord in prayer and asked Him to work things out if it would be good for both me and the guy. He knows when we're each ready and He also wants to protect us from being hurt. We're all different and really shouldn't let someone else's dating life affect how we feel about our own.

Diane, 19

You know you're old enough to start dating when you can honestly ask yourself *why* you want to date someone and you find that your motivations are long-term and for the good of both of you. You should want to date to get to know a person better or to show someone you respect, admire, and care about him or her. You should not date someone because you want to be respected, or to impress your friends or because you are physically attracted to the person. If you date for reasons like these, you will find that your relationships are less meaningful.

Shawn, 18

I think 16 is a good age to start dating, because by that time you hopefully know yourself well enough to date others. I think it's easier to develop friendships with the opposite sex if you don't emphasize dating every person you meet. I couldn't date until I was 16. I tested my parents over and over to change their rule, but they wouldn't budge. I now realize I was saved from a lot of heartache by not being able to date.

Jason, 18

ThiNk AbOuT It

What do you think is a good age to start dating? If you are already dating, do you wish you had waited longer? Do you wish you had started earlier? Why or why not?

How can you be friends with someone without the person thinking you want to date him or her?

I struggle with this a lot. I'm very friendly, so some guys take it the wrong way and start avoiding me, so as not to lead me on. I've found that it helps to be really aware of how the other person is acting. Sometimes if I *do* just want to be friends and I'm sure they have the wrong idea, I tell them. It's definitely hard to confront them, but so far everyone has appreciated the fact that I let them know where I stand. This doesn't necessarily mean going and telling every person, "I just want to be friends," but if you know for a fact that he or she is confused about how you treat him, then tell him. Another important step is to make sure your actions fit your words. By saying you just want to be friends, but always flirting with them and hanging all over them, you can cause great confusion. Treat others that you want as friends in the same way that your friends treat you.

Cammie, 18

It can be hard sometimes, but I believe it's possible. However, I have also experienced the other side of this situation. One friend of mine thought that I liked her and was looking for more than friendship. Looking back, I think this problem resulted from a lack of communication. I never let her know how I really felt, so when I was nice to her and friendly, she took that as my being romantically attracted. It really messed up our friendship. I learned, though, and with another girl I communicated with her often so we always knew what was going on with each other. Through this relationship, I have found her to be one of my closest, dearest friends. We are not romantically involved, nor do we need to be. We were able to establish a friendship without pressure or misunderstandings.

Barry, 18

Don't spend a lot of time with the person one-on-one. Make it a point to spend the majority of your time in small groups. It helps take the pressure and expectations off.

Chris, 18

Be honest with them. If they seem to believe you want more, tell them you just want to be friends. They will probably understand and you can become good friends. Just make sure that if you do want to be just friends, then that is what you act like—a friend. Don't flirt with them. It will hurt and cause confusion.

Monaca, 16

Talk to them if you're really worried. Body language can be misinterpreted, so be really careful with your actions. Don't let them think you're flirting with them.

Kelly, 17

Make sure you're not sending the wrong signals. Spend time with them, but don't spend a lot of time alone. And talk to them. Be honest with where you are. Not knowing and wondering is always worse than knowing the truth, no matter how painful.

Heather, 18

ThiNk AbOuT It

Do people sometimes misread your intentions and think you want to be more than friends? Is there anything you could be doing differently? What do you think is the best way to handle this?

I've been friends with someone for a long time. Now I find myself liking him as more than a friend but I'm afraid to tell him because I don't want to hurt our relationship. What should I do?

Be careful. Think about how important that friendship and that friend are to you. Is it worth the risk of romance to lose that friend? Test the waters carefully. But test them to see if maybe there isn't some like on the other end as well. If there is, it may be all that much easier for you. You don't want to embarrass yourself or your friend, make them uncomfortable, or ruin your friendship. If your relationship as friends is strong enough you should be able to share all your feelings and thoughts and tell the person how you feel. You should be able to talk about it, work it out, and come to a conclusion. It's a risk, but it could have good results. Personally, I really dislike hearing from someone else if someone likes me. I'd rather hear it from the person, and I'd rather he hears it from me. Remember, be careful. You can't go easily from a romantic, physical type of relationship directly back to good friends.

Kate, 18

I think if you have been friends with someone a long time you should talk to him or her about it. Explain that you don't want to hurt the relationship you have already, but you think it can become a deeper commitment. Always keep in mind that if he or she doesn't have these same feelings the friendship can still stay strong.

Mike, 18

Probably one of the most difficult transitions we have to deal with in relationships is a shift from friendship to something more. I've found in the past that it is best to just be relaxed about the whole situation. Friendship is very important, and if it is meant to develop into more, then just let it happen naturally. Don't force anything.

Anne, 19

WAIT! I can relate to this one: *Wait to see what happens.* Is this just a fleeting thing? Do you really like this person as more than a friend, or do you just like the idea of having someone to go out with? Check your motives!

Angie, 18

Talking is the answer. Let them know your feelings and see how they feel. Just be aware that if you ever break up, you may not have the same friendship again. Believe me, I know. It's really hard to still be friends. Consider the risk.

Maggie, 16

This is a very touchy and nerve-racking situation. I feel that if you two are good friends, you should be truthful about your feelings. He or she may not feel the same way, but if he is a friend you can trust, you should tell him. However, before you do, make sure you pray about it frequently to ask the Lord's approval. If He puts up signs that say "No" or "Wait," then listen! Be careful. If your feelings are getting in the way or hindering the friendship, you either need to share your feelings or back off a little. Whatever the case, don't push things. If the Lord wants a relationship to begin, it will. Remember, *pray and listen.*

Brent, 19

ThiNk AbOuT It

Do you agree that honesty in relationships is always the best? What if you're afraid that your honesty might hurt your relationship or another person?

I've had some bad experiences with relationships in the past. It's really hard for me to trust. How can I erase those memories from my mind?

I also have had some bad experiences with guys and have a hard time trusting. When I came to college I had to deal with the fact that guys were all around and I couldn't escape them. Most of my male friends know that I've had some hard times and I don't like being touched. Those memories will always be present. One thing that has helped me is to spend a lot of time around guys. I started out slow, with short times. I have grown to understand that, yes, I have had hard times, but these are totally new people and surroundings. I think you should give new guys a chance. I know it is going to be hard to trust. Most of that comes with time, so hang in there. It's going to be an upward battle to not think other guys are the same as the ones in your past, but the battle can be won.

Teresa, 19

I believe it is really hard to erase memories from your past, but you can learn and grow from them. By learning from them you can guard yourself from being put into the same situation again.

Michelle, 19

I can relate to this so well. I have terrifying memories—ones I'd love to erase, but they still exist. I tried to bury them. DON'T! They will resurface and bring back the pain again. Memories run pretty deep, but don't get discouraged. Try to deal with the root of your problem: Why don't you trust people? Sometimes you can deal with the problem, even at the root, and the trust still doesn't come right away. But I do believe that over time the trust will eventually return, though it is a process. There are a few things I think you can do to help the trust return: 1) Pray about it. Yes, it's a cliché, but it happens to be a cliché that works. 2) Before you get into a relationship, make sure you know the person really well. This makes it easier to trust. 3) If you go out, do so in groups. It reduces the risk of getting into a sticky situation, especially with the physical aspects.

Give your situation time and realize that some good things come out of it. For instance, because of my experience, I'm a lot more careful. I'm more aware of my surroundings and the situations at hand so that I can be more comfortable. I also have been able to help others with their struggles in the same area. Lastly, although I wish my experience hadn't happened, I have grown emotionally and spiritually through it. Hang in there!

Cathy, 19

I dated a girl for over a year in high school. I totally trusted her. Then I found out she was going out with other guys behind my back when I was out of town. I didn't date again for two years because I just didn't want to be hurt again. Finally I began to realize that not everyone is the same. There are people out there who *can* be trusted. I focused on friendships with girls and just kept praying that God would show me if he wanted any of those relationships to develop into more. I've been dating a girl now for six months. We are best friends and talk about everything. And yes, I trust her. We were friends for so long before we began to date that I knew her really well. That made all the difference.

Will, 19

Find the one who will be patient with you and understand where you're coming from. You may never forget the memories—I haven't. But you must keep that behind you so far as to not let it control you. Realize that not all people are like that. On the other hand, use the experiences and learn from them. It may give you a true sense of who you can and can't trust.

Sarah, 18

ThiNk AbOuT It

How have past experiences affected the relationships you are in now? What is the best way to deal with painful things that have happened? What are some things you can do to put the past behind you?

A lot of my friends are going steady with someone, but I'm not sure that's so smart. I like having a lot of friends without having that pressure, but sometimes I want the security. What do you think?

It *is* a lot of pressure to be "going steady." Being comfortable with a big group of friends is *great*. About sometimes wanting that so-called "security" that comes from going steady: It's better to wait it out with a bunch of friends than to jump too quickly into a relationship for the "security." A lot of times it's hard to be the one on the outside looking in, but how do you know you'll find security? You might just find an unhappy trap you want out of. A good question to ask yourself is: "Why do I feel the need for the security of a steady relationship?" Consider prayerfully what you choose to do, and *always* check your motives.

Anna, 18

I dated someone for two years—my freshman and sophomore years of high school. It was very much a security net. It was hard when we broke up, but I had so much fun after that just getting to know lots of guys and learning to be friends. Don't be pressured to go steady. I know it's hard. My freshman year in college everyone (so it seemed) was dating seriously but me, and I felt left out. But I made some really good friends that I would have missed out on if I had been going steady. Take your time and enjoy your friendships!

Janna, 19

It's great security—you're right. But it's not the ultimate. It can make you miserable with fear of losing the security, or you could hang on to a situation you don't really like. I dated a guy for two years just because I didn't want to not have a boyfriend. It was a huge mistake. I missed out on a lot of neat friendships because of my fear. You may sometimes be lonely, or not have a date on a Friday night, but the friends you can make and the ways you can grow as a person make it all worth it.

April, 18

You should never rely on anyone else for your security. If you don't want to go steady, don't. It's your life. You must learn to be an individual without depending on anyone else. Going into a relationship for security's sake will simply make you vulnerable. It would be a very unhealthy relationship.

Samantha, 18

Everyone, at one time or another, needs to have that sense of belonging, but if you date someone for that reason, you may be hurting yourself and someone else. That happened to me. I didn't date until I was 17. I went out on a date with a girl my junior year. I didn't really like her that much but she had a huge crush on me. It made my ego feel good and it was nice to have the "security." I dated her for a year before I finally realized it was a bad situation. I had played the game well, though, and it really crushed her when we broke up. I felt horrible. If I had been honest from the beginning we probably could have been good friends. My need for "security" really messed it up. Don't hurt someone else because of your own selfish motives.

Stan, 19

Some people are ready for steady relationships and some are not. You need to find out what's right for you—what God wants for you—then make that decision. You will only find temporary security with relationships. With God you will find eternal security. Relationships are not meant to be a source of security but a source of friendship, love, joy, support, etc. Check your heart and get to know YOU!

Belinda, 18

ThiNk AbOuT It

Do you think it's good to "go steady" with someone for security? How can you meet the needs you have without doing that? Are you under a lot of pressure to "go steady"? What is the best way to deal with this?

Is it okay to date non-Christians or should I just date Christians?

It is okay to date non-Christians—at least that's what I thought in my senior year of high school. I decided to date a friend of mine who was funny, intelligent, and enjoyable to be with. None of this brought on problems. What *did* seem to cause disputes were related to activities on weekends. I went to church on Saturdays (for choir rehearsals) and Sundays (for worship). He would understand my actions as commitments and nothing more. When I tried to explain to him that going to church was out of service to God, he didn't understand. No matter what I said during our "deep" talks, I found that he didn't really relate, no matter how many "uh-huhs" were said. We finally broke up. In my opinion, it's okay to date them, but dating Christians would give you a deeper understanding and eventually a deeper friendship (and relationship) in the long run.

Becky, 19

Although I believe the Bible says that God doesn't want Christians to marry non-Christians, this question strikes a personal note. My father wasn't a Christian when he married my mother, who was. Obviously I'm glad they married, or else I wouldn't be here. However, I also know of the pain my mom went through because she couldn't share everything with my dad. He wanted nothing to do with religion. It took a long time for my dad to become a Christian, but he finally did through many painful experiences. By looking at the hard times my parents went through I know that I only want to date and marry someone who shares my love for Christ and my commitment to Him.

Sandi, 18

From the time I was in early junior high I received great Christian teaching about how it is unwise to date non-Christians, and I agreed with it completely. When I was a sophomore I found those teachings harder to follow than I ever thought. I started dating a good friend from the track team. He was one of the nicest guys I knew—nicer than a lot of guys in my youth group. But from day one I questioned whether or not it was wise. For nearly a year I struggled. I didn't compromise my standards and I wasn't treated poorly, but our relationship remained very superficial. I could never share with him the things that meant the most to me. I was going through inner turmoil. I began to stop questioning and my spiritual life became such a game.

After a year I went to a Christian summer camp to be a counselor. There I developed the richest friendship of my life. In just several afternoon conversations with this guy, I knew him deeper than I knew a guy I had dated for a year. Why? Because I could share my most intimate thoughts with him—what God was doing in my life and what I *hadn't* let God do. We became the best of friends. I fell in love with the Jesus in him. What a difference!

Brenda, 19

I've always thought that dating non-Christians was okay. All of my youth pastors and mentors told me to date Christians, but I ignored them. I went out with a couple of non-Christians and the relationships were not glorifying to God at all. I know you don't care when you're a teenager who just wants a date, but it really *is* important. Once you fall in love, it's really hard to end the relationship. My boyfriend now isn't really on the same wavelength as I am, but I love him. I am now in the hardest position I've ever been in. You never know when you're going to fall in love. You want him to be a Christian so that your relationship can be grounded in Christ. Even though it may seem impossible to find a Christian guy, they are out there and they are the best kind. Just be patient and God will send the right guy your way.

Blair, 19

Dating non-Christians is something that can be easily justified if you want it to be. I don't think it is always beneficial, though, because they aren't making decisions based on God and the Bible like (hopefully) a Christian does. You have to date Christians just as carefully, though. Just because someone is a Christian doesn't mean he or she won't do wrong things or hurt you. It's important to make wise dating choices in general.

Laura, 19

I found that when I dated a non-Christian I couldn't tell her that God was important to me. Maybe it was my own insecurities and fear. But she could never understand who I really was until she knew how much I loved God. Also I could never really love her totally because she didn't share a common love for Christ.

Art, 19

God calls us to love everyone, so there is no harm in *loving* people, whether they're Christian or not. The problem is when the love God is talking about is misinterpreted. Love means to care about a person, to want the best for him or her. For Christians the best for another person is helping him or her know God. I think you can love someone, but if he's not a Christian, don't date him. Be his friend, pray for him, tell him about God, and support him, but don't let your desires get in the way of God's desires. God tells us to not be unequally yoked, which means to not be married or committed to someone of a different religion than you. Dating is preparation for a deeper commitment and marriage. Dating someone who isn't a Christian is leading that person on and/ or hurting your relationship with God.

Lisa, 18

If you're a Christian, I'd say date a Christian. I dated a nonbeliever one time and thought it was okay because she went to church every once in a while. However, she didn't have a commitment so her morals and values were compromised. You wind up getting in trouble when you date someone with different morals. I found that out the hard way. Luckily for me, I bailed out before I had compromised my morals.

Andy, 18

In looking for a relationship, you must look for someone who you are not just attracted to, but with whom you can share all your thoughts. In dating you are mostly in search of a deep friendship. You're looking for someone who, when responding to a situation, causes you to nod in agreement—things he likes and you like, what he believes and what you believe. Common ground is the foundation for a successful and enjoyable relationship. What could be more important to have in common than your deepest beliefs? Your love for Christ is what you are. It's what you're built upon. Date Christians and grow as friends in Christ. There is no other way to go!

Ellen, 18

The Bible says, "Do not be unequally yoked." This goes back to the days when two oxen were used to pull a plow. A yoke was used to hold them together. The oxen needed to have equal strength, because if one was weaker than the other, it would throw the whole thing off. The stronger one would be slowed down. By past experience, I can say that dating non-Christians never works, even if you're trying to bring them to the Lord. You are taking a risk at being brought down yourself, just like the oxen. The last time I tried this I ended up going out drinking with the guy and totally destroyed my witness to him. I learned from that mistake.

Carol, 18

ThiNk AbOuT It

Are you comfortable with dating non-Christians or do you think you should just date Christians? Why or why not?

Is it okay to date someone to try and bring him or her to the Lord? How can I do this?

No. When you date someone to try to bring him to the Lord, you will most likely be disappointed. If the person decides to change, he might be coming to the Lord for the wrong reason—to please you. He should change because he desires it for himself. If he doesn't change, you are stuck in a relationship that has started off for the wrong reason, plus you don't have your faith in common. I suggest remaining in the bounds of friendship while witnessing to someone; then you don't get involved emotionally and hormonally.

Bonnie, 18

My youth pastor gave a great example about dating non-Christians while trying to win them to the Lord. Picture a guy standing on a chair with a girl standing on the ground beside him. What happens when he tries to pull her up into the chair? He can't, no matter how hard he tries to pull the girl up to his level, he won't be able to. But, if the girl on the ground tries to pull the guy to her level, no matter how strong he is, she will pull him down. It's exactly like that in our dating lives. When we date non-Christians, it's easier for them to pull us down to their level than for us to pull them up to ours.

Ashley, 18

Usually we don't really date non-Christians just to bring them to the Lord. If so, we would just remain friends

and witness to them. As humans, most Christians try to justify dating non-Christians by calling it a witness. Better to be honest and just stay friends.

Meri, 19

Dating someone to try to convert him or her to Christ is a dangerous and deadly trap. It is an *effort* to maintain a relationship with Christ, but it is very easy to give in to the attractive ways of the world, to give in to the desires of your flesh. Things that feel good are easier to do than things that are good. Dating someone to bring him to the Lord may begin with good intentions, but in the long run he is probably just interested in *you* and not in your healthy relationship with Christ. The more you like him, the weaker you make yourself to giving in and letting your Christian walk suffer. Once the emotional attachment is there, it becomes extremely difficult to stay objective about where the relationship is going. The missionary dating goal becomes your excuse to do what you want.

Julie, 18

I tried it in a "solid" relationship that lasted for five months. We had been friends beforehand so she knew my faith before we began dating. She professed a commitment to Christ about halfway through the relationship but has backslidden since our breakup. A nonbeliever may claim to love Christ and/or go through the motions in order to please or impress the person he or she is dating, and not because he truly believes it. I could have saved myself a lot of heartache if I had remained friends. She might also have eventually made a real commitment to Christ if things hadn't gotten confused.

Bart, 18

Dating seems to bring a lot of heartache. Why is there so much pressure to date, anyway? Am I weird to not want to date?

Weird, no. Lucky, yes. There are certain things you're missing by not dating, but you're also avoiding a lot of problems. If you have no urge to date you won't miss it. You can have a better time going out with your friends on weekends than hassling with a date.

Matt, 16

You're not weird—you're smarter than most. Dating is often awkward, confusing, and damaging to relationships. Take your time.

Doug, 19

No, you're not weird at all. There *is* a lot of pressure to date, but getting pressured into it would be a really bad reason to start a relationship. You don't have to feel out of it just because you don't date. If you don't feel ready, or it just doesn't appeal to you yet, that's fine. There may be a time soon when you find someone you really like and might consider dating, but don't worry about it now. Enjoy where you are, have fun with friends, and deal with dating only when you want to.

Sherri, 18

When I look back on my high school years, I wish I hadn't felt the pressure to date. It just causes a lot of trouble and heartache. It is fun, but it just isn't worth the trouble it causes. You aren't weird—you're probably smart. The ideal situation would be to work at developing yourself and building friendships. Wait until you want to.

Jessie, 18

If you don't want to date, more power to ya! You're feeling this way for a reason. The American culture has implanted the "be a couple or nobody" mentality. A lot of other cultures focus on group relationships with the youth, which is a great thing. The pressure to be exclusive is more or less nonexistent. This is great because that pressure has led to a lot of bad relationships. Don't let someone else's "great" relationship get you down. What's good for him or her is not always good for you. Having a group of friends of both sexes helps you understand from the opposite sex's point of view. It creates great friendships that can lead to an intimate relationship, but if it doesn't you are still left with some great supportive friends of the opposite sex.

Erin, 18

I sometimes don't feel like dating. This is okay! When you feel like this, take the time to draw near to God. His awesome plan for your life will prevail. Be patient and relax. You will be more relaxed to start friendships and find your perfect match.

Ross, 19

—— **daTing** ——

Heartache comes with the territory. If you don't risk anything, you can't win anything. It's not wrong to be reluctant to date, but if the right person comes along, don't hesitate.

Dan, 19

ThiNk AbOuT It

Do you even want to date? What do you think of the whole dating scene? Has dating been a good or bad experience for you? Why do you think there is so much pressure on people to date?

Is it necessary to have a physical relationship to have a good dating relationship? Is the physical part necessary for there to be real love?

No, it is not necessary to have a physical relationship to have a good relationship. In fact, having a physical relationship can totally ruin a relationship. I had a boyfriend, Jeff, who I thought I was in love with. We seemed to be perfect for each other and I was convinced we were going to get married. So our friendship got really physical. At first it was okay, but Jeff wouldn't stop with just "making out." He wanted to go further. Since I "loved" him, I agreed to go along. I became attached to him. Jeff convinced me to have oral sex with him one night. I gave in, not realizing what I was doing. I began to resent the relationship because he got to the point where he was forcing me to have oral sex with him every night. If I didn't, he would ignore me or take me home.

I was a young Christian at that time and thought that oral sex was okay. The next summer I went to a Christian camp where they spoke on this issue. That summer I took my dedication away from Jeff and gave it back to Christ, where it should have been. It has taken me three years to fully get over Jeff, because of the physical relationship we had. I didn't intend or want to get as involved as I did, but our hormones took over and one thing led to another.

Now, when I enter into a relationship, I am careful to keep God in the center because He will work everything out according to His plans. Please take my advice and do not get involved in a physical relationship. The boyfriends you have now could be your friends for the rest of your life. You don't want to get together with friends about whom you know all about their most intimate body parts. Have comfortable relationships that you won't regret later on in life. Don't think you can stop at one point in a physical relationship. It doesn't work!

Connie, 19

Stay away from physical relationships. They only come back to haunt you. Every time I see another girl I am plagued by bad memories of terrible things I did. Just don't do it! Leaving the physical out forces you to increase your social skills, which will only benefit you later in life. Knowing how to kiss well or make out won't get you anywhere.

Barret, 19

Real love should work without any physical relationship at all. When you truly love someone, you love the true essence of the person that will never change—his or her mind, spirit, and personality. A person's appearance will change, so a lasting relationship must be based on something permanent. Physical relations are temporarily rewarding, but can cause all kinds of trouble when they are shared by a couple who are not in a permanent, loving marriage.

Frank, 18

I went to a school where couples weren't allowed any physical contact, but my boyfriend and I had a great relationship. I could talk about anything with him. Now, three years later, we're no longer dating but are still close friends and I can tell him things I wouldn't feel comfortable telling other people. Restraining from the physical part can develop friendships that will last.

Linda, 18

No, as a matter of fact the best relationships are those that aren't physical. When you aren't physical it shows that you both have enough respect for each other to resist this temptation. A physical relationship is one that causes loss of all respect for each other. It seeks one goal: To be physical. Wouldn't you rather be wanted for who you are than for what you have physically? A body will eventually waste away, but love that comes from the heart lasts forever. Real love is loving someone for who he or she is, accepting all his faults and flaws, and seeing past the skin to the person that lies within. If he doesn't love you for your heart, he can never truly love you.

Mark, 19

I think you can have a great relationship without having the physical part be the center. I am a very feelings-oriented person and I want the emotional bond to be there. I want to know the woman I marry inside out—not just to know she is the world's greatest kisser. I had a very fulfilling relationship with a girl for ten months (we are now good friends). During that whole time I never kissed her on the lips. It's not that I didn't want to be more physical, but now as I look back it is my heart that still thumps when I think about her—not my hormones.

Jerry, 19

I definitely do not think it is necessary to have a physical relationship to have a good dating relationship. I dated a girl for two years and all we did was kiss. Because of this we are still friends today. While I was in the relationship with her I had more respect for her and myself than in any of my relationships that were based on the physical part. You can base your relationship so much on having fun, talking, and just accepting the other person for who he or she is. Love is not based on the physical. It is based on trust and respect.

Jim, 18

Control in the physical aspect of a relationship is a great reflection of how you feel about the other person. It shows the respect you have and that you can recognize the fact that you are a creation of God and His plan is best!

Rebecca, 18

ThiNk AbOuT It

How important do you think a physical relationship is? What makes you believe this? Why do people feel so much pressure to get involved physically? What can they do to combat the pressure?

When is the best time to set physical limits in a relationship? How can I talk to someone about this?

The best time to set limits in a relationship is right when the physical activities begin to start. Tell the person that you have to talk and it's important to you, but you don't know how to begin because it's difficult. If you're completely honest with him there shouldn't be a problem.

Heather, 17

If you can see that a friendship is developing into a frequent dating relationship, there is nothing wrong with being open and honest right from the beginning about your standards and expectations about the physical aspect of the relationship. Better to get it out at the start, when it may be a little embarrassing to talk about, than find yourself in the middle of something really physical, regretting what you've done and feeling trapped. I found myself in this position because I didn't speak up, and it caused a lot of pain and frustration.

Amy, 19

Before you even get into a relationship of any kind you should know what your personal physical limits are. Once you are in a relationship you need to clearly state your boundaries. If you are too uncomfortable to discuss this with your boyfriend or girlfriend, then you have no business taking part in the actions that embarrass you. Your friend should be someone whom you are open with, and is above anything else one of your closest friends. When you fail to communicate, you only end up hurting yourself.

Pamela, 18

Setting physical limits is one of the most important things you can do in a relationship. I don't think there are any set standards of exactly when you should do it, but I firmly believe the sooner the better. I don't think you can approach the subject too soon, but you can definitely approach it too late. It's a very tough subject to talk about. There is no right or wrong way to approach it. Expect it to feel a little uncomfortable.

Callie, 19

The process of *setting* physical limits can be as dangerous as a relationship *without* physical limits. The biggest mistakes I have made in my physical relationship with girls have followed minutes after discussions about setting limits. Make a firm decision early in the relationship, but do it with as little detailed discussion as possible. A discussion of intimate acts and feelings can lead to a spirit of experimentation and lust rather than restraint and purity. Don't let your emotional intimacy grow into physical intimacy. Be candid and strict but also nondescript. This is, in my opinion, the biggest struggle of any long-term romance. Don't let your desire for intimacy endanger your desire for purity.

Adam, 19

You need to set the physical limits a lot sooner than you think you do. You have to realize that anyone can go too far—anyone. People who go too far are not always "them." You have to make sure that *you* share responsibility. It should not just always be up to the guy to initiate and the girl to decide when you're going too far. You need to both feel responsible. I used to think that if you decide in your head beforehand that nothing will happen, nothing will. It's not that easy. I am determined to go into marriage very much a virgin, but I have gone farther than I thought I would. So has she.

Carey, 19

Set physical limits as soon as the relationship starts. I have ruined three very good relationships by not talking about the physical end. Please set limits right away. It is uncomfortable to talk about, but so very needed.

Charles, 18

It's hard to give a concrete answer to the question of when. You don't want to hop into the car on your first date and start spouting off a list of "I won'ts." Each relationship is different. However, it is better to do it too EARLY than too late. Your friend should respect where you are coming from.

Kathryn, 18

The best time to set limits is before you ever enter a relationship. My first serious dating relationship moved quickly into a very physical one because not only did I not develop and define limits, but it never occurred to me that I needed to. I had a worldly view of dating and I was looking forward to a physical relationship. The Lord used the relationship and our breakup to teach me about the importance of setting limits. Physical relationships tend to end up in bed. There is a progression involved. In my own experiences I have gone from sitting on the couch snuggling, to kissing occassionally, to making out. I've come frighteningly close to having sex. Only by the grace of God I haven't.

Therefore, the best time to set limits is before it begins. After my first relationship I began figuring out how to avoid that dilemma. I'm currently seriously dating a girl who really loves the Lord. We have discussed avoiding a physical relationship and we both have set standards to avoid such. One thing that really helps us is for me not to stay late at her house. I try to leave by 11:00 P.M. (She helps by kicking me out of the house.) I've noticed in my experiences that I am weaker spiritually, and more likely to mentally let my guard down, when it gets past 11:00. I combat that by leaving at a certain time. I'm not real good at it, and that's why my girlfriend helps me. It's a team effort. You both have to work at it for it to work.

Dale, 18

ThiNk AbOuT It

Do you know what your physical limits are? Do you feel comfortable communicating them? What would you do if someone went beyond the limits you set? How would you feel about it?

How do you know when you're ready to kiss someone? Does it just happen or do you plan it?

Kissing is not a rite of passage into a relationship. It is not necessary for a healthy relationship. From my experience, kissing is not something to rush into. The kiss moves you into a whole new level of intimacy. It is nothing to fool around with. It does not *just* happen. A kiss is not like two attracting magnets that have no power to stop themselves. To some extent it is a planned move. Destiny does not give lip gifts.

Mark, 18

I don't think I have ever known if I was ready to kiss someone. I just always felt that if the relationship was important to me, I wanted to further it. As far as the question about it just happening or planning it, I have experienced both. For instance, one time afer school I just kissed my girlfriend at the time. No planning or anything. Wtih a different girl I planned to kiss her during "our song" at a school dance. I have fond memories of both situations. Neither is more important to me. It can really go either way.

Stan, 19

Believe me, when the time is right, it just happens. Don't force anything, and make sure you've set your limits beforehand, because once a move is made a lot more can "just happen."

Al, 18

Kissing should never be forced or planned. If you feel a bit uncomfortable—like it might not be right—don't kiss. It will mean a lot more if the time is right.

Pattie, 17

Usually it just happens, and when it does it's not at all as weird and awkward as you thought it would be. It's totally natural. Don't forget that the other person is probably just as nervous as you are.

Lisa, 18

Don't ever let anything in your physical relationship "just happen." My boyfriend and I talked about what it meant for us individually, where it would lead, and if we should wait before we kissed. No, we didn't plan the exact timing and day, but we had talked about it and knew where we stood on it before we kissed. Don't be afraid to talk about it first. That is such an important part of any good relationship.

Joyce, 19

ThiNk AbOuT It

How important is kissing in a relationship? When do you think it should become a part of a relationship? Why do you feel this way?

How can you know when you're ready for a serious relationship?

Good question. Last year I wasn't dating anyone and was afraid I never would. But God taught me some incredible things. Before you get serious with another human being, make sure your relationship with God is serious. Before you get comfortable with and start depending on another person, take time to learn to depend completely on God, because sooner or later you'll find yourself expecting too much from the one you're dating—things that only God can fulfill, like security and assurance. Before you get serious with someone, know that your first dependence is on God alone.

Jasmine, 19

I wish I had thought to ask that question and then answer it for myself before I started dating. I just started dating when someone asked me and then got involved in a "steady relationship." Looking back on it, I realize how much I *wasn't* ready for a serious relationship. It led to a lot of things I wish hadn't happened and it really hurt my growth as a person. I was living for someone else instead of being true to myself. I think I am ready for a serious relationship now. I have a solid relationship with God that I work at making deeper. I appreciate who God has made me to be and have learned that I deserve to be respected by others. I love myself so I can freely give love to others. I have set firm limits for myself and have seen myself keep to them. Mostly I just want to be a part of someone's life, sharing everything that comes. I am praying that God will bring the right person at the right time. I pray also that I will be the best person I can be when I finally meet Mr. Right!

Ruth, 19

This may sound crazy to some of you, but I have decided not to date until I have met the person I really believe God has for me to marry. That doesn't mean I don't have a lot of girl "friends," it just means that none of them are an exclusive thing. And I don't do any more than hug them. My parents have a really great marriage and that is what I want. I've seen so many of my friends mess up or be hurt by serious relationships. I have decided to just work on becoming all that God wants me to be. I'm having fun, developing neat friendships, and trying to equip myself as best I can for my future. I pray every day for the person I believe God is going to bring into my life. Sometimes it's hard, but I feel good about my decision. And I can hardly wait to meet her!

Chris, 19

ThiNk AbOuT It

Do you think you are ready for a serious relationship? Why or why not? What are the determining factors to know if you're ready? Do you think it's important to be "ready"?

How do you keep your relationship from making the person you are dating first in your life instead of God?

The only way I know is through discipline and dedication. You have to make a choice to place God as your number one priority. It's not always easy, but believe me, it's worth it. Take it one step at a time and work at daily committing your life to God and making time for him.

Molly, 19

This is one aspect of relationships I have dealt with practically nonstop. It's really hard to keep God first in your life when it seems like everything is revolving around this one person. The best and only way I know how to deal with this is to share your faith with that person. By doing this you are setting out clearly what is most important to you, and it helps to put things in perspective. Talking about your faith can help keep you both centered on the Lord, and through His love it can bring you even closer together.

Janie, 18

In order to keep God first in your life instead of the person you are dating, you need to rearrange your priorities. Make "dates" with God and don't break them even for the person you are dating. Tell your date that God is first in your life, and that you don't want to do anything in your dating life that would displease Him.

Diane, 18

Concentrate on God. Pray and study the Bible together. Discuss what the Lord is teaching you. Keep up your own time with the Lord, as well as with your Christian friends who can help keep you accountable in your Christian life.

Kammie, 19

A good way to keep God first is to simply spend some time each day with Him, preferably in the morning before you begin your day. Just read a chapter or two from your Bible and spend five or ten minutes in prayer. By spending time with Him instead of exclusively with your boyfriend or girlfriend, you will find that it's much easier for God to stay an important part of your life.

Maggie, 18

Ask your boyfriend or girlfriend to climb up on a cross and suffer a slow death on Friday and then meet you alive for breakfast on Sunday. The result of this hypothetical test should clear up any question about who is worth loving more.

Jeff, 18

ThiNk AbOuT It

Who is number one in your life? If you are dating, who takes first place? Are you just saying this, or do your actions reflect your beliefs? What are some things you need to do to keep God number one? Are you willing to do what it takes? Why or why not?

A Further Word . . .

Contrary to popular opinion, God is not the cosmic killjoy. He really cares about your relationships.

Romans 12:1,2	Philippians 3:12,13
2 Timothy 2:22	Romans 15:5,6
2 Corinthians 6:14-18	Matthew 6:33
Ephesians 4:17-24	1 Peter 1:22
1 Corinthians 3:16,17	1 Corinthians 6:13-20
Psalm 51:7-12	1 John 1:9
Philippians 2:12-16	1 Corinthians 10:12,13
James 1:12-17	Mark 14:38

chApTer 2

Finding Mr./Ms. Right

What do guys look for in girls?   51

What do girls look for in guys?   53

Is it possible to find the perfect person?   55

How can you know if someone would be the right one?   58

*A lot of guys seem to be immature
and unromantic. What is their problem?*   61

Why are girls so moody?   62

*Should I act differently from
from who I really am just to get someone to like me?*   64

Should looks or personality matter the most?   67

How can I tell if someone likes me?   70

Do guys mind if a girl asks them out?   71

How do I ask someone out?   74

What is the best way to turn down a date?   76

Is flirting wrong?   78

*What do you do if a guy
you like tells you he likes someone else?*   80

What do guys look for in girls?

Different guys look for different things, but I can tell you what I look for. Physical plays a role, but even more than that, I like people who are nice and fun to talk to. I also would try to find out as soon as I can if they're a Christian. That's very important. No matter how good someone looks, if she's not a Christian, or if she won't talk to me, I lose interest.

Dave, 19

Guys often get distracted looking at girls, but they value the one who is able to persist in sharing her unique traits with confidence. Often the unique traits are as simple as humor, love for God, honesty, and loving of life.

Stan, 19

I first get interested in their looks, but won't get involved with them if they have no personality. The personality will become more and more important the longer I know this person. I will not even be interested if they do not have a good personality because it dulls the conversation with that person.

Brad, 17

I look for all the physical aspects which are evidences of a healthy mental and spiritual life: a great smile; bright, attentive eyes; and a well-groomed body that is cared for. God has a strong desire to make Himself known through people. This should be clear in the way she treats everyone, not just her friends.

Rick, 18

It depends. Some guys just want sex. But there are a lot of good, decent guys out there. I'm at the point where I'm looking for someone who I can be best friends with, some-one who I can be very close to emotionally and spiritually. Basically, I'm starting to look for a potential wife.

Matt, 19

Guys like girls who are attractive to them in terms of looks. Because there are so many different guys, there is an infinite number of ways that girls can look attractive. Quali-ties that guys like are also varied. Quite often qualities such as self-confidence, humor, and sensitivity attract guys to girls.

Carl, 18

God made all guys different, and they all look for different qualities in girls. This is a good thing, or else all guys would go for the same girls. It is an unfortunate truth that the first thing a guy notices about a girl is her looks. So it sometimes seems like love is unfair. When a mature guy is looking for a meaningful, lasting relationship, though, he looks for a girl who is friendly but not aggressive, and loyal, so he can feel sure she will not suddenly leave him or chase after somebody else.

Gene, 18

I look for a certain "glow," an inner beauty that is seen on the outside. I'm not saying that my girlfriend didn't attract me physically when I met her, but she didn't become the most beautiful woman to me until I saw in her a shine, or glow, that others lacked. Where does this glow come from? It comes from Jesus. Call me corny, but girls who are more serious about loving Jesus than pleasing their boyfriend are the way to go. The most unattractive girl is a girl who has been rejected or disappointed by the person she loves most. If I am the person she loves most, she'll end up pretty unattractive. If she loves Jesus most, she'll glow with the love and beauty that can only come from loving the One who will never let her down.

Jeff, 18

What do girls look for in guys?

I look for intelligence, thoughtfulness, kindness, and nice looks, but "nice looks" can mean anything. I find that guys "grow on me" as I get to know them. A guy's generosity, thoughtfulness, etc. may shine through and make him quite attractive to me.

Tammi, 18

It's always outward appearance that we notice first, of course. There's no way around it. For me, though, outward appearance can change a *lot* when I get to know a guy. If I meet a guy who is not the best-looking person on earth, but he's funny, self-assured (but not cocky), not overcritical, and he listens to me, he looks better and better as I get to know him. It can work the opposite way, too. If I meet a really good-looking guy who turns out to be a big jerk, he doesn't look so good anymore. Most of the guys I notice aren't classically handsome, but they're sincere, honest, and fun. Here's a big tip, guys: *Listen to the girl!* There's nothing we like more than a guy who takes time to listen and who cares about what we say.

Karen, 19

The most important and attractive guy to me person-ally is one who loves the Lord with his whole heart and is not ashamed to show this to the world.

Leah, 18

I look for sensitivity, someone to lift me up when I'm down; someone who enjoys similar things, is fun to be around, is easy to talk to, and who has a sense of humor—just an all-around nice guy. Looks don't necessarily matter, but they sometimes initially make you look deeper. Guys, be yourself around us so we can see how you really are.

Jill, 16

I look for someone with strong character, who is sure of who he is and of his relationship with the Lord; who respects women and their abilities; who is fun and has a good sense of humor; and who is consistent in what he says and does.

Tina, 18

Girls look for a guy who is respectful, but not a puppy dog. Someone who is attractive, but not stuck on himself. Someone who is hilarious, but at the same time mature. Someone who is a good listener, and yet has interesting things to say. Someone who loves Jesus more than anyone else.

Jami, 19

I look for a guy who is secure in who he is, and above all has a strong relationship with God. I like a guy who is sensitive to his own feelings and can share them. He has to be honest in all areas.

Candy, 18

I tend to look for guys who I can joke with, feel comfortable with, and are physically attractive. No, this doesn't mean drop-dead gorgeous, because each girl finds different things attractive in a guy. Basically, just be yourself. I know that sounds like a cliché, but it's true. Something else I like is a guy who makes an effort to talk to me because in some small way that lets me know he's interested in me, and at least wants to be friends.

Dodie, 19

ThiNk AbOuT It

What do you look for in a person? How about making a list and putting down all the things you want in a friend? In a date? In a spouse? What are the things you won't compromise on? What are the things that would be nice but wouldn't rule someone out of the picture if he or she didn't meet them?

Is it possible to find the perfect person?

No. He was here 2000 years ago, though. His name is Jesus.

Randy, 19

No. Are you perfect? I'm not, and I don't think anyone else is either. Therefore I think you won't ever find the "perfect guy" or "perfect girl." They might be really close, but not perfect.

Terri, 18

No! I think most of us have struggled with looking for the perfect person. Only recently have I accepted the fact that there are no perfect people in this world. This doesn't mean you shouldn't have high standards when looking for a date or relationship. Just don't expect perfection because you will never find it. I think our "perfect" person should be the one that best complements who we are.

Sara, 19

I don't think there is a perfect person for you. He or she will not fulfill all your expectations or satisfy all your needs, and you cannot do that for him or her either! But you can complement each other. His strengths will build up your weaknesses and your input will challenge him. You may find many people with strengths that will complement your weaknesses; there may not be only one out there for you. But in sharing of yourself with others you will find the one you will choose to be with for the rest of your life.

Barbie, 19

No. Stop looking for Mr./Ms. Perfect. They don't exist. I've found that the beauty of a relationship is in the fact that two people who aren't perfect—who are far from perfect— come together and make each other better people. Accepting someone for his or her flaws and imperfections, along with learning to share your weaknesses with him, makes for a wonderfully rewarding relationship.

Carol, 19

No. There will always be flaws in people, even the ones you date or marry.

Chris, 19

No. But I didn't know this for awhile. For some reason I was convinced I could find the perfect girl. I would start dating someone, convinced she was the "perfect one." It didn't take too long before I discovered she wasn't perfect. Then I would end that relationship and continue on in my search. I finally learned that no one is perfect. A friend of mine pointed out one day that if I ever did find the "perfect girl," she would dump me because I am so imperfect! There are a lot of wonderful people, but everyone is human and has flaws and weaknesses. But I still believe God has someone for me. Both of us will have to work hard on our relationship, but I believe there is someone being prepared for me who will best complement who I am and who God wants me to be. I can only hope and pray I will do the same for her.

Gary, 19

ThiNk AbOuT It

Do you think it's possible to find the perfect person? Why or why not? What would be the "perfect person" for you? How would you describe the "perfect relationship"?

How can you know ahead of time if a person you like would be the right one to have a relationship with? What should I look for?

Unfortunately, it is very hard to know ahead of time whether the person you are interested in is the "right one." It does matter—a lot—what kind of person you go out with. Some things are a matter of personal taste, like whether you enjoy being with someone who is really funny, whether you are more attracted to the quiet type, or whether you fall for someone who is romantic. There are some basic things, however, that you should look for, like whether he treats you and others with respect; whether he is involved in alcohol, drugs, or any other habit you disagree with; and other basic things. Once you feel he would make a good dating partner, you can let down your guard a little and see if you would like to know him better. Although there is no set formula for whether or not someone would make a great boyfriend or girlfriend, chances are the more you get to know him, the easier it is to tell. As you date different people, you will learn from your relationship and be able to recognize things that you really liked or disliked about the people you've dated. This will help you as you get older to make the ultimate decision if a particular person is "the one" for you. Your experiences will help you decide.

Margo, 18

Sit down and write out all the traits you are looking for in a guy or girl. Someone encouraged me to do this, and it has really helped. You won't necessarily get someone who meets everything on your list, but it helped me define what is really important to me and what I won't compromise on. I've learned it's really important who I date because each person shapes a little of who I am and who I will become. I don't want to play around with that.

Elizabeth, 19

It's very difficult to know ahead of time if it will be a good relationship. You really have to start it first in order to know. It *does* matter what sort of person you go out with. As inaccurate as it may be, a reputation can say a good deal about a person. Is he known for dating a lot of people? Don't expect a long-term relationship. Does he have a positive attitude about bad situations? This might be a relationship worth pursuing. Don't expect to know right away if it will be bad or good, or if it will be a lasting relationship. Look for things that would suggest thoughtfulness, sensitivity... you complete the list for yourself. You know best what sort of person suits you.

Ardith, 18

One of the first questions I ask myself when I think about dating someone is, "Can I see myself marrying this person someday?" I believe this is a very important question that is far too often overlooked. Dating should not just be a thing to do, because too many emotions are involved. It would be a waste just to throw them away.

Daniel, 19

I think the decision of who you have a relationship with will affect the relationship more than anything you do or say during that relationship. Before you can decide what type of person to date, you must know what type of person *you* are. How do you think? What are the significant aspects of your personality? Have you examined your relationship with

Christ? How do you deal with your sexuality? Not knowing yourself will be a major strike against a relationship. Once you have a good idea of who you are, find someone who is compatible with you. This will require that you get to know him or her relatively well before you ever get involved romantically. Above all, pray that God will control your life and put you in the relationships He wants you to be in. Then try to be patient while you wait for Him to do that!

Wayne, 18

Just get to know the person as a friend and nothing more. I would be just friends for a minimum of five months to truly get to know someone. Look for someone you respect, someone you can be natural around, someone you can be serious with, someone you can laugh with.

Bob, 18

From my own experience, I had a good friendship with the person prior to our relationship. I liked her from the beginning and felt confident she would be a good person to get involved with. I think it was the trust I had in her, the ability to talk with her about anything. I believe being friends first helped me decide for sure, and eventually the relationship just happened.

Gordon, 18

ThiNk AbOuT It

Do you feel like the person you're dating now is the right one for you? What do you look for in a person you date?

A lot of guys seem to be immature and unromantic. What is their problem?

Guys are taught not to be sensitive and not to cry. Society has conned them into thinking they shouldn't be emotional. A guy has to be really secure in order to risk being romantic. Immaturity is often an effort to try to impress you! Be patient. They'll learn.

Sandra, 19

Part of this problem is that we girls have somewhat idealized notions of romance. If you notice, the ideas we get generally come from books or movies. If you look closer you'll find that the men we fall in love with are men created by women. There are romantic guys; they just have a unique way of showing it. We have to try to understand their concept as much as they should try to understand ours. Guys in high school seem immature because they have not had enough time to develop their own creative ideas about chivalry, etc. And believe it or not, we can be kind of clueless when they *are* trying to be romantic. They have to try it out before they are.

Connie, 18

People go through stages at different times. Allow people to develop at their own pace.

Dawn, 18

Many guys are immature and unromantic because they have a lot to learn. But many others are just acting that way because they're insecure and don't know how to act. So don't judge by surface appearances. Get to know them.

Jonathan, 19

When you see guys most often, is it in a group or alone? Generally, when guys are with other guys, they are rather surfacey around women. If you get the chance to go one on one, there will be a change of heart.

Bill, 18

Many guys *try* to be immature and unromantic. We have more fun with other guys that way, and we also (strangely enough) think women like that kind of behavior. Personally, I was always scared of being laughed at if I was romantic. Females, because of society's pressures and expectations, are much more easily able to be romantic than guys. Men today are seen as tough, fun-loving guys who enjoy pain and suffering.

The first time I wrote a girl a poem, I was proud beyond words. I read it to her and she laughed in my face. Then she asked, "Were you being serious? I'm sorry!" Yet all the while she kept smiling.

Ladies, please be lenient. Be willing to put up with clumsy attempts at sensitivity, and be more willing to listen than laugh. Gentlemen, take the risk. The rewards are worth slight embarrassment.

Barry, 18

Why are girls so moody?

We girls can be moody—no denying it! A lot of us blame it on PMS. That does have some effect, but it's not an all-month thing! Girls tend to be more emotional because of other hormones. Sometimes we act moody because we have learned it is a great way to get attention. This doesn't make it right, though. I have learned I can have more fun when I work at having fun instead of pouting so someone will come and hug and comfort me. There are times this really is needed, but fun times, good talks, and understanding how others are feeling are just as important.

Yes, we're moody and we tend to feed off the moods of others, so watch out, guys. Check to see how you're acting, too!

Julia, 18

Girls are moody because we are emotional beings. Lots of times we are moody due to PMS, lack of sleep, and excess stress. I am usually the moodiest the week before my period. During this time the world turns upside down. The slightest thing can set me off. I become dramatically emotional and depressed. I also crave chocolate! I have also learned to get my sleep because I'm moody when I'm overtired. I'm sometimes snappy and my temperament is difficult to control. When I'm stressed I tend to have a short fuse; I don't like to be distracted from the things that need my immediate attention.

When a woman is moody, she is sometimes undesirable and difficult to figure out. She may seem as if she doesn't want attention when what she is really saying is that she needs lots of love, support, and attention.

Ami, 18

What a question! I wonder about it sometimes, and I'm a girl! I think it all depends on the type of girl. My sister is one of the moodiest people I know, especially when it's her time of the month. You may laugh, but I know to stay clear from her when she's like that. Not all girls are moody, though. You might be mixing moody up with sensitive. Girls definitely tend to be more sensitive about things. That can be a real blessing, however. Girls tend to know when guys are hurting, how to get them to talk, how to listen, how to understand . . . There are some positive things to it!

Wanda, 18

Girls are about as moody as guys are; they just express their moodiness in different ways.

Will, 19

It depends on the girl. Some girls get moody when they're stressing about things. Some just act that way because it gets them attention from guys if they burst into tears or storm out of a room. Their self-confidence is low and that's how they reassure themselves that people care.

Crystal, 19

ThiNk AbOuT It

What are the guys like who are in your age group now? What about the girls? Do you think they will grow out of some of their characteristics? What things about yourself would you like to change? What would you like to change about your friends of the opposite sex? How do you think you should handle those things that bother you now?

Should I act differently from who I really am just to get someone to like me?

From past experience, it just isn't worth not acting like yourself to get someone to like you. I did that all through seventh to ninth grade. During those years I had about seven girlfriends, but none of them lasted more than three weeks. They just weren't good relationships. Half of those girls I only talked to at school. The other half I only talked to out of school. Being yourself just makes things easier, though it may seem not to.

Keith, 18

When I was in ninth grade, I got the bright idea that girls wanted to date scum. So I got very moody and defensive, thinking that some girl would want to be right there to solve all my problems and go riding into the sunset.

That attitude got me nothing but trouble. As I'm sure you can guess, girls wanted nothing to do with me because of my attitude. This fact simply got me madder and madder, which drove girls farther away. One day, in a moment of brutal honesty, I confronted this behavior, and I realized two things: I was not being true to who I really thought I was, and nobody really likes to be around somebody who is moody all the time. This was one of the hardest times of my life—to suddenly realize that nobody really liked me and that it was my fault.

With my Bible in hand, I began down the road back to who I wanted myself to be. What helped me most was 1 and 2 Corinthians and Ephesians. A key turning point in this process happened during my freshman year of college. I came to a Christian college and thought the girls would be like me—wanting to date like mad. After more rejections than I care to put in print, a friend dared me to go a month without even trying to date. Being naturally competitive, I agreed. I spent that month learning how to develop a solid friendship with other guys, and the importance of that. It was this turning point that enabled me to understand myself, and at this point I could effectively date.

Don't act differently for someone of the opposite sex. Try to find out who you really are and then act like yourself.

Currently I am engaged to the most wonderful girl in the world, who is also comfortable with herself and me.

Mitch, 19

If you have to act differently around someone to get him or her to like you, then you will be uncomfortable around him, and won't have as much fun. If the relationship lasts, and the real "you" comes out, your friend may not like the "real you." If someone does not like you for who you are, then that person is not worth your time.

Chad, 19

ABSOLUTELY NOT! I've always felt that if someone didn't like me for who I was, he really wasn't worth my time. In high school it was hard at times. There were people I really wanted to like me, so I chose to act differently. I think most of us do that at some time in our lives. But it's better to be yourself and not have a boyfriend or girlfriend for a while than to be someone you're not and have dates. After all, they wouldn't really be dating *you*. Be yourself, be real, and don't give in to compromise. This way you will find *real* friends and a *real* love.

Tasha, 19

I know it's a natural response to try to change yourself to meet someone else's standards, or to imitate someone who gets a lot of attention from the opposite sex, but putting on a mask is not the way to get a certain person's attention. First of all, think about this person who you are interested in. If he or she doesn't like you for who you are, is he really better than someone that God may have for you in the future who will be looking for someone *just like you?*

Second of all, God not only created your body and your mind but your personality as well, and He accepts you as you are. Some people in your life will accept you as you are and a few won't, but don't cover up the special unique person that you are just for a guy or a girl. If anything, be who *you* are with all your heart—that's what attracts people.

Mandi, 18

ThiNk AbOuT It

Do you think you should act differently than you are to get someone to like you? What do you think makes people do that? What are some ways to help them get over feeling they have to do this? Do you sometimes do this? How does it make you feel? Are you in a relationship where you are doing this now? What do you think you should do?

Should looks or personality matter the most?

I definitely think that personality should matter more than looks. I think it's important to like the looks of the person, but it's more important to like the person. It's being good friends that makes for real conversation and sharing. Also, if you are looking at a possible lifetime commitment, you need to be able to live with the person even if he or she is old, wrinkled, and decrepit.

Nancy, 18

Well, what does your gut instinct, your deep-down

heart feeling tell you? God doesn't look on the outside like people do—He looks at a person's heart. Besides, what lasts? Not *looks*, that's for sure.

Donna, 18

I think I have an advantage over most people when it comes to this question. It's very easy for me to not get hung up over looks—I can't see. I love my boyfriend for his wonderful personality, for being loving, giving, and wonderful. People tell me he is attractive, but what does that mean? His beauty is one I see with my heart, not with my eyes. That will never go away.

Amy, 19

Be real. That's what matters! Don't go out of your way to look like somebody you're not. Our society has lied to us by telling us looks are all that matters. Don't believe it. Maybe that is why the divorce rate is so high. So many people base their relationships on the physical rather than the personality. No matter who you marry, he or she won't always have the same physical beauty she had when you first fell in love. The great thing is that if you fall in love with her personality, as time goes on she becomes even *more* beautiful in your sight!

Scott, 19

Personality is so much more important than looks. Deep down inside, what do you really want someone to like about you? Do you want him to like your body, something you really can't do much about, or do you want him to treasure you as a person? Don't you want him to accept your ideas, be thrilled over what makes you laugh, and care for what you care about? "We do not look at the things which are seen but at the things which are not seen. For the things which are seen are temporary, but the things which are not seen are eternal" (2 Corinthians 4:18).

Bets, 18

Looks are usually what first attract people, but sometimes someone who is good-looking turns out to be a jerk, and the more homely person turns out to be the most caring, sensitive person you've ever met. Of *course* personality matters most.

Margaret, 18

Definitely personality. If you get married, you'll grow old with that person and he won't be that physically attractive anymore. Personality is much more dependable. *But,* be careful not to get serious with a guy you aren't physically attracted to as well. There needs to be a balance.

Sheila, 19

Let's not kid ourselves—whether you're attracted physically to a person is important. But in the long run, looks start fading fast. If looks are all the relationship stands on, it will fall fast. There is always going to be someone who looks better than the person you're with. Personality is what sustains a relationship. Even more important is that you share a love for Christ. When Christ is the center of your lives and He is reflected in your life, then your personalities can come together. Then you'll have a great center core to have a relationship on. This type of relationship can last forever.

Timmy, 18

I think, without a doubt, that personality is more important. A relationship that is to be long-lasting cannot be based on looks. It's okay to be attracted to a person's looks, but there needs to be some sort of depth to the relationship. Personality gives you a better idea of how compatible two people are. When looking for a relationship, I place more emphasis on personality because it helps you to achieve that depth in the relationship.

Grady, 17

ThiNk AbOuT It

Do looks or personality matter more to you? Why? Which do you want other people to see more in you? Are your actions contrary to what you really believe?

I think this person likes me but I'm not really sure. How can I tell?

In my view, girls today are put in a very difficult position. They are faced with the dilemma of being discreet, yet also outgoing and friendly. If you have a feeling someone likes you, don't become obsessed over it because it causes you to act differently toward the person and creates a situation that may never have existed. Work on developing and enjoying a friendship. Keep your heart open. If anything else is supposed to happen, it will in time.

Caroline, 18

Spend time with the person in groups. Get to know him and his friends. Don't try to throw yourself at him but let him know you enjoy being his friend. He will show signs. Just keep your eyes and heart open.

Mandy, 18

Just hang out with him in a casual atmosphere and get to know him as a good friend. Let time take care of the rest. Be patient. Time will tell.

Sherry, 18

Usually when a guy likes you he acts goofy and tries to joke around with you. Many times he will be annoying and act stupid, but he just wants you to notice him. As guys get older they learn how to show their interest in a better way.

Kim, 18

Some things that show you someone has an interest in you are:
1. If he spends more time with you than others.
2. When you're talking, he looks into your eyes.
3. There is physical contact when you talk (touch shoulder, hug, touch hand, etc.).
4. If he visits or calls you more.
5. If he openly flirts.

Jonna, 18

Do guys mind if a girl asks them out? Should it always be the guy who approaches first?

No. In fact, some guys even like it. Because of their personality, they don't feel as comfortable to make the first advance as some other guys do. Girls asking them out could boost their confidence and make them feel more comfortable around us.

Sara, 16

— daTing —

Absolutely not. In fact, it helps take the guessing out of dating. Surprise, but we guys don't know everything and sometimes we need a little help. There's nothing wrong with a girl expressing interest in a guy by asking him out.

Bob, 18

In the long run, I think it's better when the guy initiates. If the girl initiates, she is forever uncertain about how he really feels and if he really would have pursued her, given the chance. As an act of respect, women should wait for men to initiate.

Robin, 18

Sometimes guys mind. Often we don't. But if you really like someone, I don't think you can afford to worry about it. You might not end up going out if the girl always waits for the guy to ask.

Art, 19

Some guys mind, but most of them think it is really cool. If you want to risk it, go ahead.

Emily, 17

I don't mind usually, unless it is a very aggressive approach and someone I don't even know. That to me is a big turnoff.

Mitch, 19

For me personally, I'm flattered when a girl asks me out.

Stan, 19

Not at all. A lot of guys would like to be asked out by a girl!

Lane, 18

Here at school, we have a name for girls who ask guys out frequently: "man hunters." This is a big turnoff. If you like a guy, talk to him. If he likes you, or finds you attractive, he'll make the first move. It's best to take it slow. If you're already friends, go ahead and have a good time as friends.

Stephan, 19

Guys really enjoy having a girl ask them out once in a while. This takes the pressure off the guy, because although everyone may say it, it is not easier for a guy to ask a girl out than it is for a girl to ask a guy out.

Chris, 19

Few guys these days mind being asked out. Just remember that most guys are wimps about this. They would probably be relieved to have you ask them.

Phillip, 19

No. Please do. It makes things much easier. I really liked a girl for a year or so, but I was just too shy to ask her out. We were good friends but I just couldn't seem to move beyond that. She tells me now that she knew how I really felt but was frustrated because I wouldn't make a move. Finally she drummed up her courage and asked me out. That one simple act gave me a lot of confidence and I was much more comfortable after that. Sometimes we guys need some help to get going. I have been dating her for a year now and we have a great relationship.

Juan, 18

I personally love it when girls ask me out. It takes the huge pressure off me. I don't think it always has to be the guy who approaches first.

Seth, 18

ThiNk AbOuT It

If you're a guy, has a girl ever asked you out? How did you feel? How would you feel if one did?

If you're a girl, have you ever asked a guy out? How did it go? Would you do it again? Do you feel it's inappropriate for a girl to do that? Why or why not?

How do I ask someone out? I really like this person but I don't want to look stupid.

Just do it! As a girl who doesn't get asked out, I don't think you could look stupid.

Anne, 19

Find something to do that you think both of you would enjoy, something that doesn't necessarily require too much talking. Be really easygoing when you approach this person. If you pretend this person is your best friend—someone who completely understands you—you shouldn't feel stupid. Also, you may never know what the person thinks of you unless you seize this chance. And don't be pessimistic. Thinking he or she will undoubtedly think you "look stupid" is ridiculous. He may be flattered that you would consider asking him out to spend time with you. As I said before, take the chance. If he means something to you, take the time to get to know him better.

Judy, 18

That's a great question. I think everybody is scared of rejection. I usually wait awhile because I'm scared, but if the feelings persist I usually act upon my desire to date this person. I just screw up my courage and ask. Thinking about it is always harder than actually doing it. The only way to find that out, though, is to try it! Go for it!

Brandon, 19

Make sure you have a pretty good idea that the person you are asking out likes you. You can almost always tell because of her flirtatious behavior or by the amount of time you spend with her in conversation. Believe me, if she likes you nearly as much as you like her, she won't care how you ask her out. She just wants you to ask her out!

Matthew, 19

You don't have to make it a formal-type date. It might be easier to get started informally. Just ask her to go with you when you run an errand, go to the mall, or go jogging. Be casual about it. When you become more confident that the person really enjoys being with you, asking for a more formal date will be much easier.

Gene, 18

There is no "stupid" way to ask someone out. If you're too shy to say, "Will you go out with me?" write the invitation in a letter or card and send it to the person. You'll feel more comfortable as you do it more. It can be hard to ask, but I promise it gets easier.

Ryan, 19

—— **daTing** ——

There are a lot of ways to ask. My advice is to make sure she knows you're asking her on a "date." I had been good friends with a guy in high school for a long time. We had done a lot of things together in groups and just hanging out with each other. One night he asked me to go to dinner at our favorite Mexican restaurant. As far as I knew, it was just another hangout time. When we got there, the manager made some crack about our "big date." I laughed and responded with, "This is *hardly* a date!" My friend didn't say anything, but I saw the hurt look on his face and it confused me. I found out later that he really *was* taking me on a "date" and wanted our relationship to be more than friends. I felt so bad but I was also a little mad because he hadn't let me know that. It would have helped to know his intentions.

Ginger, 18

ThiNk AbOuT It

What have been some great ways people have asked you out? What have been some real turnoffs?

I've had people ask me out that I don't want to date. What is the best way to turn down a date?

Be honest. While they might be disappointed, being honest and telling them that you just don't want to date them is usually the easiest and most painless way of declining. Most people appreciate honesty.

Molly, 18

From my experience, be straight with the person. Tell him (gently) that you are not interested in dating him. I had a guy pursue me for a year because he never quite got the hints I dropped. I should have been straight from the start. I would have saved myself, and him, a lot of hurt and frustration.

Mattie, 19

I know it's hard, especially if he is asking you to your face, but the best thing to do is just say no. If he values your friendship he will still be friends. It may be a little awkward at first, but you can work through it.

Karla, 17

"Thank you for asking, but I don't like you in that way." Just be open and honest.

Steve, 18

Honesty is definitely the easiest and most painless in the long run. There was a guy last year who wanted to date me but I wasn't really interested. He asked me out every week for six months. I made up every excuse in the world, but never told him the truth, so he kept coming back. I kept him hoping even though I never intended to go out with him. I was scared to tell him that I wasn't interested, and I didn't want to hurt him. I realize I was hurting him more by stringing him on, and I wasn't helping myself much either. Finally I just told him the truth. It took a long time, but now we are friends again. I think honesty is always best!

Jamie, 17

ThiNk AbOuT It

What are some good ways to turn down a date? Are there some things you can say that hurt less than other ways?

Is flirting wrong?

Flirting is playing with someone's emotions. With some people it's harmless. With others it really hurts. So play it safe and don't do it.

Jenny, 18

Flirting is not wrong unless you are doing it at someone else's expense to make yourself look good, or are leading someone on who is interested in you, or are just trying to feel important or liked, or are too physical in your flirting.

Bonnie, 19

It's relatively harmless until it gets out of control. If you give members of the opposite sex the wrong idea or make them feel alienated by your behavior, you've gone too far.

Wanda, 18

Flirting can be a lot of fun and is not always a harmful thing. The biggest problem I have with flirting is that it's shallow. I can spend an hour flirting with someone and come away knowing nothing about him aside from a glimpse at his cute sense of humor. Flirting so often blocks paths of deeper communication—questions and answers to who the person is beneath the heart-melting smile.

Cindy, 19

Flirting can sometimes be harmful. Usually the safest scenario is when best friends can flirt and know they're not really serious. That can be fun and allow for a very casual relationship. But when you flirt with people you don't know very well, you can't tell how they're going to take it. It's all too easy to take flirting seriously and think there's something behind it. Too much flirting can also earn you a reputation you may not want. Just be conscious of when you flirt, and be aware of how well the other person knows you. Flirting can be fun when you both know it is just flirting and not "advancing."

Ginger, 18

Flirting is fine as long as you're interested in the other person. If you're not interested, I would call you a tease and advise you to stop.

Bo, 16

Flirting is not wrong, but remember to watch what you say and do. It can be harmful if you flirt insensitively. Girls, watch your body language. You say a lot with your body that you don't want us guys to interpret the way we do.

Sam, 18

Flirting leads a person on and therefore you should not flirt with someone unless you really do like him or her.

Ronnie, 18

ThiNk AbOuT It

Do you consider yourself a flirt? Do you think there have been people hurt by your flirting, or do you think it's harmless? Have you ever been hurt by someone else's flirting?

daTing

What do you do if the guy you like tells you he likes someone and asks you to pray for their relationship?

You pray. Love is not selfish; it does not seek its own way (read 1 Corinthians 13). If you really like him, you'll care enough to want what's best for him, even if it hurts you.

Jerri, 19

Pray for their relationship! I know a woman who was a guy's friend all through high school. While she remained single, she helped him through all his relationships, many with her friends. Finally he realized he could talk to her like nobody else and he really loved her. They are now married. Obviously this may not happen to you, but you never know. I encourage you to give this guy to the Lord. If he's for you, it will come around. It could be great that you aren't in a relationship now. Maybe you both need to get older and more mature.

Lisa, 18

Pray for him. Pray for God's will to be done. If their relationship is right, pray for strength in overcoming your own feelings and for their well-being. If it is wrong, pray that they will realize it quickly and that all will work for the best. Above all, concentrate on how God sees this and what is best for all concerned, not just what you want. That's hard, but it can be done!

Kathy, 19

Take this as a sign that he really values you as a friend and values your opinion. It's also a pretty good sign that he doesn't like you "that way," so you need to think about just being the friend he wants you to be. And for goodness' sake, be nice to the other girl when you see her. When you pray, pray for him like he asked you to, and not for yourself that they will break up or something!

Meri, 19

You pray. Pray for God's will in the situation. And also pray for God to guide your own heart, because it's hard to pray for something you don't really want to happen.

Linda, 18

I love this question! I had the very same thing happen to me. I really liked this guy but he started liking a friend of mine. When he asked me one day to pray for them I thought I was going to die! The only reason I did it is because I told him I would and I didn't want to be a liar. I can't say they were fervent, heartfelt prayers, though! I really struggled with my feelings with him. That was what kept me going back to God. Gradually God changed my heart. I'm convinced it was because I spent so much time praying. I see him as just a friend now and am happy for the relationship he still has with my friend. So pray! You might be surprised at what God will do with your heart!

Tina, 18

ThiNk AbOuT It

Have you ever had someone you like show an interest in someone else? What would you do if that happened to you?

A Further Word...

God wants you to spend the rest of your life with Mr./Mrs. Right.

Proverbs 13:20	Psalm 1:1-3
Ephesians 5:15-17	Philippians 4:6-9
Psalm 37:1-6	Philippians 2:1-11
Hebrews 12:1-3	Romans 8:31-39
Jeremiah 29:11-13	Philippians 1:6-11
1 Peter 3:3,4	Proverbs 31:30

chApTer 3

There's Nothing to Do Around Here!

What are some fun things I can do on a date?   85

What is the perfect first date?   87

Does the guy have to pay for everything?   89

Is group dating better than pairing off?   92

When you group date, is there a good size for the group to be?   95

What are some great ways I can show the person I'm dating that I really care about him or her?   96

What are some fun things I can do on a date? I'm sick of movies and I don't have a lot of money to go out to eat.

- Go to a lake, get a canoe, find an island, and have a picnic.
- Go for a bike ride.
- Go to the fair.
- Get movies or funny films from the library.
- Help out at a service organization together.
- Go out for coffee and talk.
- Go for a walk, or jog, or swim.
- Go to a free concert.
- Have someone cater a meal for you.
- Cook together.
- Go to a park, swing and play.
- Walk in the woods.
- Watch people in the mall.
- Drive and explore.
- Go ice skating.
- Go grocery shopping together and cook a meal.
- Run errands for your moms.
- Go to the zoo.
- Take your kid brother or sister for a shake.
- Take rolls of pictures, then make an album together.
- Carol your friends in July.
- Plant a garden, take care of it together, and enjoy the harvest.

- Take a coin flip trip. For every stop you come to, flip a coin to decide which way to go. Tip: You may need a map to get home!
- Look at old family albums.
- Go to an airport and people-watch.
- Go out into the country and explore old, abandoned houses. Tip: Don't take anything; it's stealing!
- Take the dogs for a walk.
- Visit an elementary school and play on the playground.
- Get all dressed up and have a candlelight dinner in your family room.
- Go to a card store and "give" cards to each other.
- Split a bag of conversation hearts, each giving appropriate ones to the other.
- Go to a nice restaurant with live musicians and just order appetizers or dessert.
- Go to a neat museum.
- Go to a historic site.
- Go down a nature trail.
- Hike for the day.
- Chat on a beach, count the stars, and look for shells.
- Philosophize under the stars, sharing your dreams and ideas.
- Make chocolate chip cookies.
- Take Ben & Jerry's ice cream wherever you go.
- Go sledding.
- Go on group dates to Wal-Mart and have a scavenger hunt.
- Guys, surprise your girl by fixing her dinner and inviting her over.
- Take a drive up to a place that overlooks the city at night.
- Wash your parents' cars.
- Go to school plays and games.

- Go to the town pool.
- Go roller blading.
- Play board games or cards.
- Put together a puzzle.
- Go apple picking.
- Carve pumpkins.
- Do a Bible study.
- Learn to play a sport together.

A compiled list

Just be crazy, spontaneous, creative, and willing to try anything new!

Allen, 18

You want to have good, fun times, but not necessarily expensive times. Go somewhere you can talk and get to know each other. Develop a friendship as well as a relationship. Movies don't do a lot for communication, do they? Spend quality time together, talking, laughing, and playing. Those are memory builders.

Martha, 19

ThiNk AbOuT It

What kinds of things do you do on dates? Do you really feel like you're getting to know your date better through your activities?

What is your perfect first date?

My perfect first date would have to be a romantic dinner in a nice but not-too-expensive restaurant. Then we would take a walk along a waterfront, browsing in shops. Following that would be a carriage ride around the city, looking at the stars.

My other ideal would be a picnic in the countryside after a bike ride to get there. We would sit and talk by the riverbank, and then fly a kite together. Just a good, informal time of getting to know each other.

April, 19

My perfect first date would be a time to really talk to the person and get to know her as a friend. A quiet setting, a relaxed atmosphere, no pressure—the activity doesn't really matter.

Joe, 19

A date where we could spend a lot of time talking together and having fun. Nothing fancy—just a place where we could relax. The perfect ending would be a simple hug. I often initiate it by saying, "Before you go, I'll give you a hug." It takes the pressure off him when he's trying to figure out if he should kiss me and it takes away the awkwardness of saying goodbye.

Pamela, 18

I just experienced my perfect first date! A friend and I decided to ask out two of our guy friends that we are kind of interested in. We wrote out invitations for a specific night, telling them they had an all-expense-paid date. We all got dressed up so they thought we were going to a fancy restaurant. Then we took them to a nearby pizza place. It was their favorite restaurant. Then we went back to the dorm and watched a movie. We all had fun and they were touched that we thought it all up.

Margo, 19

My perfect first date would be talking as friends and getting to know each other in a public setting. This puts off a lot of the romantic pressure. I experienced this with my present boyfriend. It was good to get to know him as a friend and an encouraging man of God first.

Ronelle, 18

ThiNk AbOuT It

How would you describe your perfect first date? Have you had one? What made it that way? Did you tell your date?

Just because you're going out, does the guy have to pay for everything?

Definitely not. Although tradition would suggest that the man always pays, most girls don't mind paying at least sometimes. A good suggestion is having the girl plan something (maybe as a surprise) and take the guy out once in a while. In my experience, most girls don't let you pay for everything. Perhaps if the guy pays for dinner, she'll pay for the movie, or something along that line.

Brent, 18

This question is one I have often struggled with. Being the guy, I often feel compelled to pay for everything, especially at the beginning of a relationship. Yet my girlfriend often wanted to pay. I feel it's an individual thing. Once my relationship with a girl has grown, we often split the cost of dates or she'll pay.

Greg, 18

No, simply because a relationship is for two to share. It shouldn't be one-sided by any means. The best illustration is marriage. Does the man always provide? Certainly not; he often needs help, which is what makes a relationship so beautiful. Two people share together.

Gary, 18

The guy should value the woman enough to want to pay for her in as many ways as possible. However, on occasion if the woman wants to pay the guy should allow her to.

Tim, 19

No. In this day and age girls earn just as much as the guy. I've always offered to pay after we've been on a few dates.

Kay, 18

No! Neither party should have to pay all the time. In more serious relationships, I would expect to share in finance, and would also be looking out for fun things to do that don't cost money.

Janie, 19

I think it depends on the kind of relationship the two of you are having. Many couples that start out as friends are comfortable going Dutch. On more formal kinds of dates, it shows responsibility and courtesy in a guy who thinks enough of a girl to spend money on her. When guys gripe about the amount of money they're spending for dates, we girls feel more like a burden than a friend. However, ladies, simple math says that over time a dating relationship can become expensive. The solution is to spend time doing creative things that don't cost so much. Girls, don't expect fancy dinners every weekend. Guys, if she's worth going out with, she's worth the cost.

Pamela, 18

The guy doesn't *have* to pay, but it makes me feel more useful in a way.

Todd, 18

I'm really traditional and I feel very uncomfortable when a girl pays. Some girls like to pay and some don't. It isn't an issue that's worth the trouble.

Kerry, 19

Guys shouldn't have to pay for everything. It is a generous gesture on their part to want to, but it could make them go bankrupt.

Sandi, 19

Definitely not! It's great fun to take a guy out every so often. It shows him you care about him and aren't just using him for his money. I love taking guys out sometimes. Planning and preparing for a date every once in a while also gives you a greater appreciation for the work and money your boyfriend puts into dates.

Sue, 19

Not at all. It may give the guy an extra sense of security in his feelings of ability to "provide" for someone, but nowhere is it written in stone that he alone must pay for everything. If the girl feels like paying for a date and she offers, then by all means she should feel like she can pay for it without it being a problem. In my own relationships, I like alternate paying for dates with whatever guy I happen to be dating at the time. It takes some of the pressure off both of us and doesn't leave either of us feeling like we owe each other anything.

Virginia, 18

I don't think so at all. I loved being able to treat my boyfriend to a night out every once in a while. He payed for a majority of our dates because he really wanted to, and was kind of embarrassed when I would pay, but I know he really did enjoy being treated. I encourage girls to take their boyfriends out once in a while. I think we should want to. Who doesn't want to do nice things for people they care about?

Gwen, 19

ThiNk AbOuT It

What do you think about the money issue? Have you and your friend talked about it? Should you?

Is group dating better than pairing off? Is it more fun? What can we do?

There is a different kind of fun with group dating versus pairing off. Group dates are relaxed, exciting, and fun. There is a lot of conversation and joking around. Pairing off is more intimate and a time to get to know each other on a one-on-one basis. Both are fun and necessary for the relationship.

Sally, 19

I definitely think that group dating is the way to go, especially at the beginning of forming relationships. If more people are around, it allows for better conversation and less of the awkwardness common on first dates. If you aren't comfortable with the person you're with, there are others around who can offer support and who you can talk with. Toward the beginning of a relationship, problems can happen if you don't know the person. Date rape occurs often these days, and even sexual abuse, because a guy wants something that you don't want to give. In a group, people are around, so this problem is less likely and it gives you a chance to get to know the guy really well and be comfortable with him. Later, go out on "paired-off" dates, when you know the person well and can be comfortable. Group dates are great fun. Bowling and movies have an added excitement to them when a big bunch of people are laughing and goofing off. And there are a lot of games (capture the flag, sports, ultimate Frisbee, cards, board games, etc.) that need more people to enjoy them.

Chrissie, 19

There are stages in a relationship when you want and need to be alone, but it's wise to not be alone too much. It leads to things. Groups are fun and keep you from living in your own little world like some couples I know.

Tom, 19

Pairing off is fine after awhile, but group dating offers much less pressure. Take your time to get to know the person as a friend before pairing off.

John, 19

Group dating is really fun and it helps the progression go much more smoothly from friends to more than friends. When you're with a group you aren't as tempted to get into physical things which can really cloud your relationship if they come in too early. Plus you develop other important friendships at the same time.

Star, 19

Group dating is *much* more fun on a first date than paired-off dating. First, when you date in a group there aren't the awkward silences often experienced on first dates. Also, in a group you get to know all the people, and have an opportunity to see how your date relates to others. Through group dating you will also be able to tell if your date is possessive, as well as finding out if he or she likes to have fun. Good ideas are scavenger hunts, bowling, and going out for a meal, but not a movie because you don't get to know the person.

Tonya, 19

Group dating can be much more fun, and a way to make a lot of good friends. There is much less pressure to start a relationship with just one other person. There is also no temptation to get physical, so your relationships become more meaningful and less risky.

Scott, 18

Do both. Group dating is a blast, but don't listen when people say pairing off is evil. You have to have time alone with your boyfriend or girlfriend, but don't be afraid to do the group thing either.

Sean, 16

Groups are not always better. It's true that groups may be less awkward at first, but they don't often give a true picture or provide real depth. I'd rather go in a pair. After the original uncomfortableness, you have a chance to get to the true base of each other.

Doug, 19

When you group date, is there a good size for the group to be?

The group should be small enough to allow everyone to talk and react together but also still be couples if it is an official date.

Suzanne, 18

I think it depends on what you're doing, but I'd say generally four to eight people. Less than that and it's not really a group date. More than eight can sometimes just be confusing or cumbersome when trying to get everything and everybody organized.

Diane, 18

Bigger than two, but not an odd number. Make it as big as you can get people, transportation, reservations, and activities for. During my senior year, 12 of us went on a group date to our midwinter dance and had an absolute blast! It was easily the most enjoyable dance I had throughout high school.

Robin, 18

I think six works out well—three couples. That way you can have fun together as well as share some meaningful conversations with everyone getting to talk.

Joan, 18

If you're not really dating but just wanting to hang out with a bunch of your friends, then I think you should go for an odd number. That relieves the pressure of feeling like you have to pair up with someone.

Ben, 19

I think a good size for group dating is six to ten. You want a group that is big enough to do group activities—like scavenger hunts, board games, playing sports, etc.—but small enough so that you can talk to everyone and get to know them.

Angela, 17

If you're going out just for fun, make sure it's an odd number. That way there would be no chance of everyone breaking off into couples.

Janie, 18

ThiNk AbOuT It

Do you think group dating or paired-off dating is better? Why? What are the benefits of each? The drawbacks? Do you think there should be both? Is there someone in your group of friends who would be good at starting activities for groups?

What are some great ways I can show the person I'm dating that I really care about him or her?

- Affirm him! Look for good things about him and bring them up.
- Build her up, especially in front of other people.

There's Nothing to Do Around Here!

- Run errands for him when he's busy.
- Dedicate a song to her over the radio.
- Ask him how he's feeling.
- Call him at home after he leaves your house to make sure he got there.
- Give her a note.
- Give him a Hershey's Kiss or Hug.
- Bury a treasure and make her a treasure hunt map to find it.
- Tell him you care.
- Make dinner for him.
- Sing to her under her window.
- Give him flowers.
- Buy him his favorite sandwich at Subway.
- Kiss her nose.
- Write a poem.
- Hold her hand in front of your friends.
- Stop when she says to.
- Cook dinner, then get your family to serve it.
- Buy him his favorite CD.
- Slip a note in her notebook.
- Send him thank you cards for special times.
- Call her and sing, "I just called to say I love you!"
- Never forget birthdays or anniversaries.
- Throw him a surprise party.
- Meet her at the airport after she's gone somewhere.
- Listen.
- Give lots of hugs.
- Watch football with him.
- Go to the ballet with her.
- Help him study for a test.
- Clean her room.
- Make him a box of memories (ticket stubs, photos, etc.).
- Be available.

There's Nothing to Do Around Here!

- Be respectful to her parents.
- Take his kid sister to the mall.
- Pray with her and for her.
- Send him a card.
- Give her your jacket or your favorite shirt that she loves.
- Go to church with him.
- Write the fairy tale of your relationship.
- Massage her feet.
- Make him cookies.
- Spell her name out in rose petals on her front porch.
- Give her a teddy bear.
- Do his laundry.
- Hold her hand while she gets a shot.
- Buy him a plant (it can symbolize the growth of your relationship).
- Visit her when she's sick.
- Make a tape for him.
- Put together a collection of poetry that says how you feel.
- Make a list of the way she affects your life and give it to her.
- Learn new ways to say I love you:
    "You make me smile."
    "You make my day brighter."
    "You mean a lot to me."
    "Thanks for being you."
    "I care."
    "You are special to me."
- Go to his sports events and cheer him on.
- Give her little gifts for no reason at all.
- Tell him often that you appreciate him.

A compiled list

—— **daTing** ——

ThiNk AbOuT It

Does your friend know how much you care for him or her? Do you think you need to show this more? How do you feel when people do special things for you? Do you consider yourself a "giver" or a "taker"?

chApTer 4

Are We Really Supposed to Talk?

*My boyfriend and I only talk
about shallow things. How can we learn
to communicate on a deeper level?* 103

*My girlfriend and I talk a lot
but I have a hard time sharing my feelings.
Are all guys like this? What do I do about it?* 107

My boyfriend and I only talk about shallow things. How can we learn to communicate on a deeper level?

I always wondered that too. I'm not the best communicator, but I wanted to talk about more serious things than the weather. I remember my older sister coming home and telling me how she and her boyfriend talked openly to each other. I couldn't even imagine doing that. It wasn't until this year that I started to. I have a hard time openly communicating my feelings and thoughts. The first step was that I learned to trust my friends here at college, as well as the guy I eventually started to date. I was able to trust him because I slowly got to know him without even the intention of dating him. As our friendship grew, so did the feelings. It takes time. Start out first just getting to know the person. At first it might be really shallow. I wasn't able to tell him some deeper things at first. It would have made things awkward. I'm not sure exactly how it happened, but as time went on we shared more and more with each other. It's the same way you get to be close friends with a girl. Your boyfriend should be your good friend. It takes time.

Kristin, 18

If you are physically active and spend quite a bit of time together but only talk about shallow things, you need to end the relationship. Relationships are built on friendship and trust, which need to be established first. Get to know a guy and become friends *first!*

Arlene, 19

Try praying together. There is something about sharing prayer requests and bringing them before God together that will open up deeper levels of communication.

Patty, 18

Play ten questions. He asks ten things he wants to know. You must answer, and then you switch roles. Questions can range from "What is your favorite color?" to "What is your most vivid childhood memory?" to "What character trait do you admire the most?" Persevere. It takes time. Also, look at why you don't communicate. Is there no time because you're too physical? Does the other person not listen well? Understanding can be helpful.

Belinda, 18

Make sure that talking about things comes before intimacy. When you allow intimacy in your relationship, this becomes more interesting to you than knowing about your boyfriend's life. Also, how about opening up to him first? Even if he doesn't ask you, tell him how you feel about certain issues and then ask him what he thinks.

Sara, 16

Learning to communicate is not a quick process. You have to be willing to take risks and to ask the tough questions you have on your mind. You are right in being concerned, and I think that is the first step. Hopefully, he feels a similar need for deeper communication and will respond. I think he would be flattered to realize that you truly want to know who he is and what he thinks about things. Don't expect the discussions to jump from what your favorite class was that day to what you have never shared with anyone. Be patient and don't give up. If the relationship doesn't work out you will still have learned how to build friendships.

Julie, 19

To deepen conversation, I've learned that sometimes the best thing to do is ask good questions. Good questions are those that are creative and thought-provoking. They should elicit more than simple yes or no answers or short-phrase responses. Adding "why" to the end of a question helps the other person to explain himself. As you listen, think of other questions that can show you more about the person. Choose something he is interested in; look for what lights up his eyes as he talks or brings a smile to his face. Be sure to also have a running list of things you're interested in. Use these things if there is an awkward pause or the conversation leans too heavily on your partner's side. The deep thoughts will come as people feel more open to share with each other.

Carrie, 19

Ask questions. Steer away from the shallow things. Talk about dreams, pains, fears, faith, relationships with family, etc. Listen and show interest in his responses so he will feel free to open himself up to you.

Margo, 18

I'm sure you've heard before that a true relationship is built on trust. Well, it's true. You have got to go out on a limb. Try telling him something of meaning to you, something you are concerned about, and trust that he will take you seri-ously enough to care. A relationship, like any living thing, has to either grow or wither and die. If your relationship with your boyfriend does not grow, does not cause you two to become closer, you will instead grow apart.

Crista, 18

Try to throw some topics into your conversations that are intense. You be the one to put forth effort into communicating on a deeper level. If he doesn't respond, or insists on staying shallow, then most likely he is just plain shallow. If this is the case you should try looking elsewhere for a meaningful relationship, because good communication is the most important aspect of any dating relationship.

William, 19

I think the best way to learn to communicate is to just spend a lot of time together. Also, just start sharing little things with him. Guys usually have a hard time sharing their feelings. But once you give them a little subtle push they usually come around. Be sure to spend some time in prayer about it.

Mac, 18

Are you vulnerable with each other? When one person tells the other person something that is hurting him, it can make the other person able to relate. Everyone has hurts. To hear someone share a problem that no one else knows creates a bond. Knowing that you go through problems too, and that you trust this person enough to share it, leads to vulnerability on his part as well.

Thad, 19

It's really frustrating when a relationship feels like it's at a standstill because there is not good, valuable communication. I've found that the key is honesty. Communicating may be one of the most difficult things to tackle, but it is a major foundation for holding a relationship together. Honesty also means being vulnerable with the other person. I know it's hard to open up sometimes because there is always potential for hurting your friend, or being hurt yourself, but that's the risk you must take.

Laney, 19

ThiNk AbOuT It

How would you rate your ability to communicate? If you're not satisfied with it, what do you think is blocking it and causing the problem? Are there things you can do to make it easier and more fulfilling?

Is your physical relationship causing a breakdown in communication? What do you need to do about this?

Do you ever pray together? Do you want to?

My girlfriend and I talk a lot but I have a hard time sharing my feelings. Are all guys like this? What do I do about it?

I don't think all guys are like that. My ex-boyfriend and I talked about anything and everything. He shared his feelings with me more than I did with him. All you can really do is build up enough trust in the relationship to be able to communicate. Don't try to be so macho about your feelings.

Joanie, 17

My boyfriend had a very hard time sharing his feelings with me or anyone else. The fact that you know this is a problem is awesome. I think a lot of guys have this problem because "guys aren't supposed to show emotions." You need to get in touch with your own feelings first, then try to share these. Tell your girlfriend you know this is a problem and are trying to work on it. That will make her more patient with you. Ask her to help you share your feelings; this will help her feel a lot more included and will let her know you're really trying. That makes all the difference.

Millie, 18

You're not unusual. Many guys have a hard time sharing feelings. I would spend more time with your girlfriend on walks. That has always helped me. Evening walks, especially, seem to loosen my tongue and bring out great ideas. These are sometimes the best times to talk.

Jimmy, 19

Not many guys are lucky enough to be able to naturally share their feelings with others. As you grow closer to your girlfriend and your relationship becomes more meaningful, it should become easier and more rewarding.

Rob, 18

Guys are generally brought up to conceal their personal feelings. Usually it isn't until a girlfriend comes along that someone really wants to hear their true feelings. Guys have to get used to this. I would suggest that a girlfriend share some of her feelings first to set the tone. Then she could ask questions like "What do you think about that issue?" or "Have you ever felt like that?"

Gerald, 18

Are We Really Supposed to Talk?

Most guys do have a tough time sharing their feelings. Try being honest and telling her you have a tough time with this. Ask her to help you. You can suggest that she ask you more questions about what she wants to know. It may really be hard at first, and you may stumble over your words at first—I did—but it got easier with time. Now it feels natural to share what I'm thinking and feeling. But I definitely needed help.

Derrick, 18

Guys are naturally more closemouthed about their feelings. It's just not cool to show them. I've found that I have to just take the bull by the horns, go out on a limb, swallow my pride, and spill it. Once you get one sentence out it gets easier. If your girlfriend knows your feelings she'll be better able to understand you. It will cut down on misunderstandings and fights.

Ned, 18

I am a girl but have dated many guys in your situation. I have encountered, dealt with, and overcome this problem with several of them. First of all, not all guys are like this. To put all men in a single category, no matter what it is, would be like saying all music sounds the same. Everyone is an individual with his own strengths and weaknesses. Sharing your feelings may not be one of your stronger points, but that doesn't mean it can't be. Trust, I believe, is the key factor in being able to open up with someone. Build trust with her and be trustworthy for her. Let her know your heart—all that you think, feel, experience, and believe in. Tell her that she is the only one that you trust enough to share these feelings with. Ask her to ask you probing questions that you can share your heart about. If you two truly love and respect each other, then keeping confidences will come naturally.

Knowing this will help you to feel more comfortable with each other, and you will start to share more easily and naturally.

Eileen, 19

ThiNk AbOuT It

Are you willing to make yourself vulnerable to someone else? Do you think you should be able to? Why?

Do you trust the person you're with? How does that make a difference in your relationship? Do you think you should keep a relationship going with someone you don't trust?

How do you feel when people really want to know how you feel and ask you questions? Why?

---

chApTer 5

But I Can't Make Up My Mind!

*Is there anything wrong
with dating more than one person at a time?* 113

*I'm dating someone, but I really like
someone else, too. What should I do?* 114

*How do I tell someone
I just want to be friends?* 118

*I have been dating someone for about a year,
but on vacation I went out with someone else.
Should I tell the person I am going steady with?* 120

Is there anything wrong with dating more than one person at a time?

There is nothing wrong with *casually* dating more than one person. It's an opportunity to learn about different people and about what kind of person is best for you. The key is that there is total honesty—that your dates are aware of your commitment level and involvement with others.

Paul, 18

Not at all. Just keep your options open and let all of them know that you're not dating them exclusively. If you become serious with one, though, you should probably tone down on your other dating so as not to create problems.

Steve, 19

No. I think dating is what you do to find out who you want to get serious with. If you date a number of different people, your odds are better that you will find the right person for you.

Seane, 16

No. If the relationships are "just dating," it's fine to date several, but be above board and let each one know. If one becomes more than "just dating," you better call off the others.

Allen, 18

As long as you are not seriously dating all of these people at once, I don't think it is wrong. Be honest with them all. Maybe even tell them you're dating around and that you're not looking for anything serious.

Becky, 19

There is nothing wrong with dating more than one person at a time. You're young and you need to see who's out there. You need to experience your options before you can find the one you want to spend the rest of your life with. Otherwise you might just settle for second best.

Kara, 17

That depends on how you define dating. If it's dating with commitment, no. If it's casual dating, then sure—go for it!

Liz, 19

_____ ThiNk AbOuT It _____

How do you feel about dating more than one person at a time? Would you mind if you were dating someone who was seeing more than just you? Why? Do you think you need to date a lot of people to see who is out there?

I don't want to lose the person I'm dating, but I think I would like to go out with another person as well. What should I do?

I believe honesty is the best policy. Honest communication is so vital! Tell the person you're dating that you really care for him or her, and that this is different and scary for you, but that you would also like to date others at this time. Most importantly, keep God as your focus. Put your life in His hands and ask Him to show you His will in the situation. Remember Romans 8:28, "All things work together for good to those who love God." In dating, it's important to find out what you're looking for in a mate.

Mollie, 19

I went through this same exact experience just a few months ago. I struggled so much with what to tell my boyfriend, who I was in a long-distance relationship with. My feelings for my boyfriend were so jumbled up that I had no idea what I really felt for him. I decided that by dating other people it would either assure me he was right for me or else assure me he was wrong. I prayed about it and then I told my boyfriend the honest truth. God really prepared his heart. I was worried he would take it the wrong way. At first he struggled with it, but he thought about it a lot and understood. You need to experience getting to know other people of the opposite sex so you will know what you want in a mate. That's something that will help you in the long run. It sure did help me straighten things out!

Alexandria, 18

I have been in this situation from both ends—wanting to go out with someone else, and having a boyfriend want to date someone other than me. Unfortunately he handled his feelings for the girl in the wrong way and cheated on me. That causes a lot of hurt, so I'd suggest that if you are unsure, be honest with both people. The longer you let feelings grow unknowingly, the longer and tougher the breakup could be.

Lisa, 19

My first suggestion would be to pray about it. Ask God what He thinks you should do. However, you may have to work with God on this one, or He may want you to use your own judgment and learn from experience. My second suggestion would be to explain to the person you're dating that you really care about him or her a lot but you're also interested in someone else, and in order to find out who is right for you, you need to date the other person as well. If he agrees to still date you or stay your friend, great! If he doesn't, remember to do what is right for you before worrying about hurting others.

Christi, 16

First of all, I think it's important to realize that you don't have to feel guilty about liking someone else. Honesty is one of the greatest things we can take to relationships. Talk to the one you're currently dating and let him know how you're feeling—that you're interested in building friendships with others. It may bother him, but you need time while you're young to figure out what you're looking for and who you're compatible with. It's also fun to build friendships with a wide variety of people. You may find that you come back to the one you are dating, but give yourself a chance to find out if that is what you really want. Always be honest with others and never fear expressing what you feel.

Sharon, 19

Look at your motives for wanting to date the other person. Are you not satisfied with your current relationship? Are you not having fun anymore? Are you worried that you're missing out on something? Do you really connect with this person? Are you afraid of committing yourself? Are you being pressured by friends?

Then examine your motives for not wanting to lose the person you're dating. Why are you with that person in the first place? Is the relationship growing with time? Is it helping you grow as a person? Are you afraid of being on your own?

Answering these questions may help clarify your true feelings and lead you to an answer. Be honest about your motives.

Cora, 19

This is a tough situation. In my first year of college I met a very exciting guy, but was still attached to my boyfriend at home. I balanced the two as long as possible, but that got hard because I wanted to kiss the new guy but felt I couldn't. I had been with my boyfriend for over a year, really believed I was in love, and had discussed marriage. But I saw the new guy as my "ideal"—he sang, he danced, he was hilarious, he was a great conversationalist, and he was a senior! Both are committed Christians. Finally I broke it off with my old boyfriend and went all out for the other. As it turned out, it scared the new guy half to death. He had never had a girlfriend before and shrank from our relationship. I realized I had been infatuated with the ideal in him and had ignored the steady love from my boyfriend at home. I ended up hurting my old boyfriend and breaking my own heart as I made a fool of myself. But my boyfriend took me back after many apologies. I don't know if this really fits the question, but it's a principle I learned: Stick with the one who sticks with you—he's your real friend. Just because someone looks perfect doesn't mean you'll click.

Bonnie, 18

There is nothing wrong with being interested in other people at this point. I would sit down and explain to the person you're dating that you are young and have lots of time before you have to get serious about relationships, and that maybe dating exclusively is not such a great idea.

Micki, 19

How do you feel about the relationship you are in now (if you're in one)? Are you content, or do you want to experience more? Can you communicate how you feel? Do you feel trapped in your present relationship? What do you think you should do about it?

There is this person who really likes me, but I just want to be friends. How do I tell him?

When I was 16, I had a girl I considered to be a friend, but then her friends told me she thought we were going out. I decided it would hurt her less if I told her myself, instead of letting time pass and leading her on. I called her and talked for awhile, and eventually told her that I valued her friendship very much, but that friendship was all I felt for her. She was disappointed, but I made it a point to show her I valued her friendship by talking to her at youth group and inviting her when large groups of us went out. I also took extra care to not do anything that would be considered flirting toward her. In a few months she invited me to the prom, and I went with her as friends. I still have a friendship with this person and there is a complete understanding between us. You must not just *say* that "we can be friends," you have to *show* that you are a friend.

Nance, 19

It is important to be honest with this person. Tell him or her right from the beginning how you feel. Don't get into a relationship that you don't want. It will only cause problems.

Neither of you will be satisfied in the relationship. Even though it might hurt the person, it is better to let him know how you feel.

Grace, 19

It will hurt the person to tell him. You can't help that, but he needs to know and deserves to know. I was in this situation once. I know I should have talked to him, but face-to-face communication like that is so hard for me. So I wrote him a note. I communicate much better through writing. It may not have been ideal, but at least I let him know how I felt. Later we talked about it and it was okay. I just needed to take the initial step on paper.

Sally, 16

If you just want to be friends, the best and safest way is to politely and kindly tell him so. Being honest is important. Try not to use the "I just want to be friends" line. Be original. Make sure you have a justified reason for not wanting to date this person. That way, if he challenges you, you will have a concrete reason.

Anne, 17

The best way to tell someone is face-to-face, but this needs to be something you feel comfortable with. A letter would also work, if talking is too hard. If you've tried the usual ways, like not always sitting next to him, or trying not to be alone with him, and he still doesn't get it, then talk to him. Just tell him you enjoy his friendship but you're not interested in a deeper relationship. Make sure you give him time to talk, too. It helped me once.

Becca, 18

There is no easy way to tell someone who likes you that you just want to be friends. There is no way not to hurt the person, but as soon as you make the decision that you want nothing more from the relationship, you should tell the person. The more you prolong it, the harder it is going to be. How do you tell him? Be nice, but don't lead him on. Just tell him you have a great friendship and you don't want to ruin it by getting into a more serious relationship. You would rather just keep things the way they are. It's always hard, but you need to tell him. This way you won't lose a good friend out of the whole situation.

Stephan, 18

ThiNk AbOuT It

Have you had times when friends wanted to be more than that? How did you handle it? Do you feel you could have handled it better? What would you like to do in the future in that same situation? How would you like someone to handle it if he or she were the ones not wanting more than friendship?

I have been dating someone for about a year. While I was on vacation I went out with someone else. Should I tell the person I am going steady with?

Yes, honesty must be kept at all times. If he were to find out from another source, it would be bad!

Debra, 19

Definitely. If you are honest it will save problems. If you are open about what you do, he will be open about what he does, and you'll have a healthier relationship. Otherwise these little things come back to haunt you.

Scott, 18

I think you should tell the person because he deserves to know. I think he would learn to trust you more because you were straightforward and honest with him.

Sunny, 18

I had this happen to me a few years ago. I had been dating a guy for a year when my family went to the beach for a month. Everything was okay until the last week. I met a really nice guy on the beach. We spent a lot of time talking and I liked him a lot. Two nights before we left, he asked me out. I had already thought about what I would do if he did. I liked him so much that my boyfriend at home just wasn't enough to keep me from going out. We had a great time! There was no physical contact at all. We went out the last night I was there, too. It was just a summer fling, though. Neither of us expected to continue when we got home. I had to decide what to tell my boyfriend. Was I going to be honest, or just not say anything? I was sure no one else knew what had happened. I finally decided I couldn't stand the deception, so I told him the truth. It hurt him, but we worked through it. We both realized that we're still young and don't need to feel like we're in a trap. It put a new freedom in our relationship. We still date, but it's not necessarily an exclusive thing. I've only dated someone other than him one time since the summer, but it's just nice to know I have the option.

Caroline, 18

Tell him. Think how much harder it would be if he heard it somewhere else. Honesty is the most important thing in the relationship. Without it everything falls apart.

Bev, 18

Honesty is the best policy. Even if it may hurt to tell him the truth, it's better than walking around with guilt or shame.

Anna, 19

Your conscience should certainly be telling you to tell the truth. A relationship can't be built on lies; it's bound to fall. If you really love each other you can probably work it out. My question is this: "Why did you cheat?" If you were fully content in your relationship you wouldn't have had any desire to cheat. So maybe you should evaluate this relationship and what it means to you.

Sarah, 18

"Do unto others as you would have them do unto you." I think the Golden Rule is pretty applicable here!

Eric, 18

ThiNk AbOuT It

Would you tell your boyfriend or girlfriend if you had gone out with someone else? Why? How would you feel if the situation were reversed? Is honesty always best in a relationship?

What do you feel about the whole issue of "going steady"? Do you like the idea of your relationship being exclusive? Why? Do you feel pressure to be in that kind of relationship? What is best for you at this time in your life?

A Further Word . . .

God wants to help you with your decisions.

Proverbs 2:1-11	James 1:5-8
Psalm 32:8-10	Galatians 5:22-26
1 Peter 2:1	Philippians 4:6,7
1 Peter 5:6,7	John 16:33
Psalm 23	Psalm 139
Ephesians 4:22-25	Psalm 51:6

chApTer 6

The Parent Thing

Why do my parents
worry so much about my dating?   127

Why do my parents care who I date?   130

Should my parents meet my date?   132

What if my parents
don't like the person I'm dating?   135

Should I tell my parents
everything about my love life?   139

Why do parents worry so much when their children date?

As I see my sister beginning to date, I really understand why my parents worried so much about who I dated. I love my sister and I want her to have the best high school experience ever. I want her to have fun. I don't want to see her hurt, and I don't want to see her compromise her values. I think that's the same way parents think. They love you and want the absolute best for you in everything, including who you date.

Carl, 18

I think parents worry, or overworry, because they have been through dating themselves. They know the pressures and they know your weaknesses. Because they want what they think is best for you, they don't want to see you hurt or in bad situations. Also, this is maybe the first time as a parent where they feel they have no control over you.

Barb, 19

Parents worry a lot because they really care about what happens to you. Your mother gave birth to you, and your parents have watched over you through every stage of your life. They changed your diapers, watched you as you took your first steps, and watched you leave on the bus for the first day of school. Your parents have nurtured you from the day you were born. They love you and want the best for you.

—— **daTing** ——
127

They worry because by the time you start dating, you're starting to make decisions on your own. They just want you to make good decisions.

Leah, 19

Because they have been there and can remember the hard times they had before they found that terrific someone they are now married to. If your parents were never married, or are divorced or separated, that just makes them worry more. Dating can be great or horrible. The mountains are very high and the valleys are very low. Parents just don't want to see any pain come your way.

Leon, 19

Parents get pretty attached to the people they give birth to and live with for 18 years—us kids. Just think how much you'd worry if someone wanted to borrow something that had been very special to you for a long time. I'd worry a lot if someone wanted to take the ring I got from my grandparents for my sixteenth birthday out for the night. It's kind of the same way with your parents.

Edie, 17

I think parents worry about their children dating because they know what is going on in people's minds. They understand the temptation of sex and they worry about their kids falling into its trap. Also, a girl's parents might worry, with good reason, because they realize that many guys are just looking for sex. Rape, coerced sex, and many kinds of abuse (physical, emotional, and sexual) are all very real and scary possibilities. I know that if I ever have a daughter I will worry about her tremendously because I understand teenage guys all too well.

Phil, 19

Would you worry if your kid left with someone you don't know much about, to do who knows what? What if they get into a car accident, get mugged, or get raped? What if her date is awful to her and hurts her heart? *Parents love their kids!* They want them safe. Sometimes it's hard to let go. It's easier if they know the people you're with, the times, and who's driving. They like to hear, "Yeah, we had fun—I had a root beer," when you get home. Do what you can to make it easier for them.

Cheryl, 18

Parents worry when their children date because dating is a serious activity. It is one of the first major things we do that can change our lives forever. Dating can lead to sex and pregnancy, STDs, marriage, or many other things. Your date can change you in many ways. Your values and goals can change quickly.

Scott, 19

Parents worry when their children date because they love them. That may sound like a cliché, but it's the truth. Parents know what can happen on dates and they want to protect you. They've been your age before and they know what *they* did at your age. They want to stop you from making the same mistakes they did. They really do have your best interests in mind, although sometimes they may seem to go too far. The fact that your parents worry is a good thing because it shows they really care about you. I have friends whose parents have let them run wild, and they feel very unloved and uncared for. So, as obnoxious as it may seem, be thankful they care!

Erin, 18

ThiNk AbOuT It

How do you think you will feel when you are a parent and your kids begin dating? What kinds of things will you worry about? What will you wish you had talked about with them before they started dating?

My parents make such a big deal out of who I date. Why do they care?

Think of it this way: Imagine you have a brand-new car that is your favorite color and that you wash and wax it every week. Some stranger comes to your door and says, "That is some car! I would really like to take it out for a spin. Could I?" Would you let him? Of course not! You'd probably hesitate to let even your best friend drive that car. Yet you are much more important to your parents than any car. Their concern for who you go out with is a big reassurance of how much they love you and want to protect you from getting hurt. Many kids in this country would give anything for people in their lives to love them and look out for them. Use these disagreements with your parents as a way to get to know them better and to find out what kind of a guy or girl *they* think you should date.

Lacy, 18

They *care* because of date rape. They *care* because of broken hearts. They *care* because of car wrecks. They *care* because of drinking and drugs. They *care* because they love you. Take it as a compliment.

Gretchen, 18

The Parent Thing

Amazingly enough, I don't know much, especially about how to run my life. I think I know, but I don't. I first realized this when I noticed my 11-year-old brother doing things I did when I was his age. As I see him doing those things I realize how easily he could hurt or even kill himself. But when I was his age I didn't think anything could hurt me, especially those same things he is doing. I now see how ignorant and foolish I was. But my thoughts and ideas haven't changed that much. I still think the things I do are fine. I wonder if I'll see my younger brother at 18 doing the things I'm doing now and think how stupid it is. Well, odd as it may seem, the response I will probably have is most likely very similar to how my parents react to me now. I think I'm wise, but my parents are more so. If you apply this to dating, most likely your parents, and mine, know best. They know if someone is good for me. If you and your parents disagree on this, try asking them why. You and I have a lot to learn from our parents. They only want us to be happy and to have what is best for us.

Larry, 18

Parents worry because they are so protective of their families. They worry about whether their kids are choosing the right people to date, ones who have morals. I'm glad my parents worry about who I date because I would rather have them worry than not care at all. Even to this day, even though I'm a college freshman and don't have my dad there to ask my date a zillion questions, I still inform my parents on who I went out with this weekend. I tell them as much information as I can about him. I think this puts my mind at ease that I have my parents' approval, even though I have the ultimate say in the final decision.

Betty, 18

ThiNk AbOuT It

What things would you like your parents to handle differently concerning your dating life? How would you like them to change? How would you like to handle dating in your own kids' lives?

Should my parents meet my date?

I think it's good for your parents to meet your date. It's courteous to both your parents and your date. Your parents may not worry so much if they know who you're going to be with. This will help build trust in you and hopefully lead to more freedom.

Flo, 18

Boyfriends and girlfriends will come and go, but you will have your parents for better or for worse. If you start dating, your parents should meet him. I know they're probably dying to meet that special person. Despite what you may think, your parents are smart people and may have some words of wisdom about your date. Don't worry if your dad tells corny jokes or your mom acts too protective. Let them meet your date anyway. They're bound to meet him sometime!

Jan, 19

They should. It lessens the distance between them, even if they don't become good buddies. It shows real respect for your parents and shows confidence in your date.

Doug, 19

I think it's really important that your parents meet your date. For one thing, it lets them feel like they're still part of your life even though you're growing up. It also tells you a lot about your date. If he is willing to meet your parents, he will be more likely to treat you with respect because he had to earn the right to take you out.

Evelyn, 18

Yes, they should. For a relationship to be healthy you need to be open, not only to each other, but also to others. If you feel like you need to hide something, then something probably isn't right. If you feel your parents wouldn't approve of your date, then maybe you should reexamine that person and determine what it is that's not right.

Amber, 17

When I'm open with my parents about who I date the result is a protection that is really helpful, even if not always appreciated! The time I tried to have secretive relationships I ended up doing things I regretted. The same is true for the girls who didn't make a point of introducing me to their parents. Relationships with girls are fun, but if you think you can manage on your own successfully, you're wrong.

Jeff, 18

I think it's really important for your parents to meet your date. I felt more secure with the guys I dated in high school because each one had talked to my parents and knew their rules. My parents knew my date a little better and were more comfortable letting me go out with him.

Stacey, 19

I am in the middle of the "parent interrogation" thing now. My parents will not let me go out with someone until he has come to the house and had the "talk." The first few times it happened I was mortified and sure the guys would never want to see me again. I guess it depends on your parents. Mine are really cool. They ask very blunt questions and are very direct about what they expect, but they also make the guys feel comfortable and show they like them. I've been amazed, but all the guys I have dated really like my parents and have appreciated the "talks." They admit to being nervous beforehand, but all of them are still friends with my parents. And it is a nice feeling to know my parents care that much. It also is great knowing the guys know the rules and have agreed with my parents to honor them. It takes a lot of pressure off me.

Vivian, 17

I've always valued my mother's opinion and know that she has good common sense. We can't always see things in other people, so it's nice to have an objective viewpoint. I found that my mother was usually right. I may have hated it at the time, but I grew to love her advice and acknowledge that she really just wants the best for me.

Corrie, 18

As a guy, I always make it a point to go in and meet my date's parents. In fact, I made a decision to not take a girl out until I meet her parents. If they are not going to be home the first night I ask her out, I'll change the night of the date. It just makes me feel better and I think it makes the parents less suspicious. I also make a point of taking my date by my house at least by the second date. A lot of time the girl's parents get to meet the date, but the guy's parents go a long time without ever laying eyes on the girl he is dating. I think it's just a nice thing to let my parents share in this part of my life. Besides, my parents are pretty cool. I like people to meet them. They have told me how much they appreciate it. Think about it, guys!

Brandon, 18

_____ ThiNk AbOuT It _____

Do your parents always meet your date? Why or why not? Are there things you or your parents could do to make it easier and more comfortable for you? How would you feel as a parent if you didn't know the person your kid was dating?

My parents don't like the person I'm dating and have told me not to see him anymore. What should I do?

I never used to value my parents' opinion about dates until I stopped to think about all the guys my mom didn't want me to date and I dated anyway. For some reason my mom always knew more about guys than I thought. All the guys she warned me about were the ones who ended up hurting me. Some of the guys she approved of hurt me also, but the majority of the time she was right. Now I'm dating a guy who is a real man of God. I was scared of what my mom would think of him because of his long hair and very casual look. However, when my mom met him she fell in love with his heart for Jesus. She was able to look beyond his outward appearance. Parents deserve more credit than we give them. I suggest you really listen to your parents and pray about whether this is best for you.

Jean, 18

I would tell you not to date him anymore. Having my parents on my side means a lot to me, but I guess it would have to depend on how close you are to your parents, and if they have good reasons for you. I would first sit down with my parents and ask them to tell me the reason they don't like me dating the person. Then take it from there.

Aaron, 18

Talk with your parents and figure out why they don't like your date. If they have good reasons and forbid you to see the person, then if you are living in the same house with them, you must obey their wishes. Your parents love you and only want the best for you. They have experienced life and most likely know what is best for you. Obey their wishes. *Do not go behind their backs;* it never works. Probably the relationship won't work out with the person, and you would have lost your parents' trust, too.

Darlene, 18

I had this very thing happen to me. I had been dating a guy for about four months when my parents told me they didn't want me to see him anymore. I freaked. When I asked them why not they said they had been hearing bad things about him and didn't want me to get hurt. I found out later that some kids had started rumors about him that eventually got around to my parents. I prayed about it really hard and then asked my parents if they would be willing to talk to my boyfriend. My boyfriend was really nervous but he agreed. Not only did he want to keep dating me but he also wanted to let them know the truth. They talked for a long time. Afterward my parents felt much better. It actually worked out great because my boyfriend and I grew much closer and also because in some of the things they talked about he changed and became an even more special person. My first reaction was to just ignore my parents and continue seeing him behind their backs, but I'm glad I didn't do that. Talk to your parents. Work it out. They might be right. Be open to it!

Karen, 19

I think it depends on what age you are. If you're in junior high or high school, then I think your parents have a better judgment. But if you're in college, then I think you're old enough and mature enough to make your own decisions.

Lisa, 16

You should recognize that your parents probably have a good reason for disliking your friend. Breaking it off will show your parents that you have respect for their advice. In turn they will probably have more respect for you and your decisions. Being apart for awhile may make your parents' view change, or maybe you'll be able to see why they were right in the first place.

Marti, 17

This is a tough question. I can only tell you what happened to me. My parents are not Christians and are both alcoholics. It's hard to have a lot of respect for them even though I do love them. They don't like the fact that I'm a Christian so when I started dating a guy who is a preacher's son, they had a fit and demanded I not see him anymore. He was the nicest guy I had ever met! I cried and yelled. I talked to the youth minister where I go to church. I prayed a lot. Even though it was hard, I broke up with him. I felt I needed to obey my parents, simply because they are my parents and the Bible says I should. It wasn't like they were telling me to do something *wrong*; I just didn't want to do it. I think they were more surprised than I was when I told them I had broken it off. Things have gotten easier at home since then.

The Parent Thing

Neither of them are Christians yet, but they have quit giving me a hard time and actually seem to respect me now. I actually saw my mom reading the Bible the last time I was home. And now that I'm in college I have a great Christian boyfriend. It was hard, but it was worth it.

Nancy, 18

Parents—mine, anyway—have this annoying tendency to be right. I dated a guy who I thought was great, but my father despised him. After the guy broke up with me—yes, *he* dumped *me*—Dad and I talked about him and explained to me why he didn't like him. He didn't tell me not to date him anymore. I actually did date him again for awhile until I realized that, as usual, Dad was right. It's hard to accept the idea that your parents don't like someone you think is wonderful. What you have to accept is that your parents love you like crazy—otherwise they wouldn't care—and they don't want to see you get hurt. You can choose either to listen to them and deal with hurting yourself or to ignore them and take a chance on the person you're dating. I personally would listen to Mom and Dad. If I had, I wouldn't have wasted half my summer after my senior year, or jeopardized my friendship with my best friend.

Rhonda, 18

I can totally relate to this question. I dated a guy for nine months. My parents told me I couldn't date him, but I did anyway. I sneaked around behind their backs, and I had to lie to them all the time. It was terrible! I felt torn between trying to please my boyfriend and my parents. I was angry at my parents for trying to tell me what to do.

Now, when I look back on it, I see how right they were. Your parents have had a lot more experience than you have. Whether you like it or not, they might actually be able to offer you some good advice. Even if you think your parents are totally wrong, think about your priorities. Is the person you're dating really more important to you than your parents, who have sacrificed their whole lives to raise you? I realized from my past experiences that my relationship with my parents is worth sacrificing a temporary dating relationship. I'm lucky: My parents and I have become closer since I broke up with him.

Wendy, 19

ThiNk AbOuT It

What would you do if your parents told you to stop dating someone? Why? What might be some of the consequences of your decision? Would they be worth the decision?

My parents think they should know every aspect of my love life. I don't mind telling them some things, but should I tell them everything?

Be open with your parents. Show them that you respect them and don't have anything to hide. If they feel they can trust you they will stop bugging you. I've heard it said, "When your kids tell you what happened on a date, there's no need to worry—it's when they don't tell you what happens that you should begin to worry!" Show your parents that you respect their concern and interest.

Betsy, 19

Parents have every reason to be worried about their child. Take it from the point of view of a mother who has carried you in her womb for nine months, and has done everything in her power to bring you up in happiness. Now you are dating! That is a shock. They're seeing their child grow up and become independent. That is really hard for parents. Be compassionate with your parents, but also let them know that if you don't tell them everything, it's not because you don't love them but because you feel you are becoming more independent and would like some privacy. Just be careful not to argue about it. It's not worth fighting over.

Allie, 18

No, I don't think your parents should know everything. Discuss with them that maybe you feel some of this information is private and personal. Tell them you're afraid the minute you don't answer something they ask, they're going to assume you did something wrong, and that might not necessarily be true; you just don't want to volunteer the information. Maybe you could talk about trust, too. Ask them how you can develop their trust in you so this won't be a problem. Talking a lot can really help.

Sally, 16

You don't have to tell your parents everything, because they don't need to know everything. Tell them you know they're just trying to protect you and want to know what's going on in your life. Let them know that you need to be your own person and that you will tell them about the big things, but that they don't need to know everything.

Kristine, 16

I make it a point to tell my parents something about every date I go on. I don't share what I consider private unless I really need their advice or input, but my willingness to tell them about things makes it easier. They feel like they're still a part of my life and it keeps communication open. There have been some times when I really needed their advice, and because of the communication there was a natural channel for me to get it.

Keith, 17

I sat down with my parents one time and asked them how much they told *their* parents when *they* were dating. They laughed and admitted they were pretty closemouthed about things. That simple thing did a lot to help. I talk to them about most of my dates but they don't pressure me to tell them things I don't volunteer. I know I can go to them if I need to, and they know I realize that.

Clay, 17

Tell them everything! My mom used to wait up for me after dates and drill me. I loved it because when I was on the date I always had in the back of my mind that my mom was going to ask me what I did and I was going to have to tell her. Besides, it improves your relationship and your parents respect you more.

Rosie, 18

ThiNk AbOuT It

How much do you tell your parents about your dates? Would you like to talk to them more? If so, what do you think blocks your communication? Is there anything you can do to make it better?

A Further Word...

God cares about teens and the "parent thing."

Ephesians 6:1-3	Proverbs 4:20-23
Proverbs 15:31-33	1 John 3:18-23
1 Peter 2:18-23	Colossians 3:12-17
Colossians 3:20-24	Proverbs 15:5

chApTer 7

Where Are the Brakes on This Thing?

How can I tell the person
I'm dating I only want to be friends?   145

My dating relationship seems
to have taken over my life. What should I do?   147

What if I feel like the
relationship is getting too serious too fast?   151

The person I'm dating is
possessive and jealous. What can I do?   153

How can I tell the person I'm dating that I only want to be friends without hurting him or her?

There's really no way around it; to tell someone he or she can't have a relationship in the way he wants to is going to hurt him to a degree. Your best bet is to be quick and honest. Don't beat around the bush; honestly tell the person how you feel. Don't wait forever. By postponing your decision you'll just add to the hurt they will feel.

Mike, 19

No matter how you say it, it will hurt. I've been on both sides, and each time either or both of us wound up in tears. It's one of those things that just has to be done. If you want to be friends, realize that it will take awhile for your friend to accept that, but if there is love you'll both bounce back. Don't stay serious just because you don't want to hurt the other party. You'll be miserable and you'll be living a lie.

Angie, 18

To be frank, there is no way not to hurt someone when you are breaking up with him or her. Be honest and kind, but acknowledge the fact that there will be some hurt involved.

Tommy, 18

Which would be worse—to keep dating him even though you don't still like him that way, or to just tell him honestly how you feel? The best thing to do is to put yourself in his position. What if you were dating someone who didn't like you *that* way anymore? Would you want to know? Just be kind and considerate. Don't talk about it to other people; keep it private. Be honest and make an *effort* to maintain the friendship. The person will inevitably be hurt; there is no way to prevent that. Just make sure you're doing the right thing. That's all you can do.

Rochelle, 18

Be honest with him. Tell him how you really feel. Most importantly, after you quit dating, treat him like a friend. Don't use the "I only want to be friends" line on someone if you really don't even want to be friends.

Susie, 16

It will hurt no matter how you tell him; so just tell him. Don't tell a bunch of garbage either. Tell him the truth *only!*

Candy, 16

I really don't think you can break up with someone without a certain amount of hurt being involved. The best way to do it is just flat-out tell him the truth. I'm not saying you need to be mean; just tell him how you feel and why you feel that way. Be as honest as you can.

Janna, 19

You probably won't be able to avoid pain altogether. Be honest with him and explain your feelings. That's the best way to avoid hurt feelings. It hurts more if he feels like you're hiding something or if he discovers it on his own. Most people appreciate honesty and can understand much better when it is used. I've broken up with two guys and had a guy break up with me. It hurt at the time, but I'm friends with all of them now. I'm convinced that honesty is the reason for our continued friendship.

Laura, 18

This is hard because of the stigma that goes with the phrase "I just want to be friends." Everyone groans when they hear these words. I would suggest that you be completely honest. If that means using the cliché, then use it. But follow it or precede it with an explanation. And don't avoid him after this. Let him know you still care. Keep acting like a friend.

Bart, 18

ThiNk AbOuT It

How would you want someone to tell you that he or she just wanted to be friends? How would you want him to act toward you after that? Have you done the same things in your relationships in the past? What could you have done differently? Are there people now that you need to talk to or act differently toward?

I've been dating someone for a year. I really love him but he seems to have taken over my life. What should I do?

When I started dating my current girlfriend, I had the same problem. We spent all our free time together and I never saw my other friends. It got so bad that my best friend came over to my house, stayed and talked with my family, then got up and left. He never even said "Hi" to me when I walked into the living room. At that point I had to explain to my girlfriend that I had to spend time with my best friend, and I had to explain to my best friend that I would be spending time with my girlfriend. After many hurt feelings, it all came out okay. It did take some work to get all parties to understand, though.

Ed, 18

I think it's very common for a dating relationship to slowly start to monopolize your time. It's happened to me before and it's a tough situation. I remember feeling torn between my friends and my boyfriend. There is a fine line that needs to be drawn. It's hard to decide how much time should be spent with each. I'd suggest trying to integrate your time if you can. Try to find things you can do with your other friends *and* your boyfriend or girlfriend. Also, try setting aside time each week for both of them.

Bonnie, 19

Talk to him. Never let one friend take over your life so that you forsake your other friends, most of whom you've known much longer. Your other friends will resent it and you will be unhappy.

Lonnie, 19

That kind of relationship is really dangerous. Unless you're ready to live with that kind of submission for the rest of your life, get out!

Julie, 17

Whoa! I did the same thing. Even if you really care for someone, you're not married yet. How will you grow as a person, or in your relationship, if there is no new input? What if you ever break up? Where will all your other friends be then? How would you feel if a boyfriend used you only between relationships? Think about it from your boyfriend's point of view, too.

Fran, 18

When I was in high school, my best friend became a Christian. He was the only friend I ever had that I saw come to Christ. It was great! Soon after this I started dating a girl. I blew off all my friends, including him. I didn't realize how hurt he was by this. Now he is far from his original faith. I'm still hurt and he is pretty messed up. Don't neglect your friends. It hurts to realize I played a part in where he is now. You have to find balance.

James, 18

Try to set aside one night a week for your other friends as a starter. Then, when you get used to that, try to get at least two nights a week away from each other.

Diane, 16

If you feel this way, talk to your boyfriend and explain that you need a little time with your other friends, too. Maybe on the weekends go out with your friends one night and your boyfriend the other night. This will prevent him from taking over your life.

Dottie, 17

Talk to her about it. You have to deal with these kinds of problems, or the relationship will suffocate. I know it's hard, but you have to in order to save the relationship.

Marcus, 19

You're just looking for an excuse to stay in an unhealthy relationship. It will be a bit painful for you, but you need to break up. It will cause even more pain if you continue on the same path. An exclusive relationship is not a healthy one and causes damage to both parties.

Carla, 18

I dated a guy for nine months. When we broke up, I had no friends. The next time I dated a guy for 2½ years and we were really careful. We only went out once or twice a week. We really enjoyed being together, but we wanted to build our other friendships, too. When we were together we appreciated it more and had more to talk about.

Eileen, 19

ThiNk AbOuT It

If you are in a relationship now, do you think it is a healthy one? Do both of you make time to spend with other people? How would you rate your other friendships? Are they important to you? Are your actions supporting your beliefs? How would your friends answer that question?

Are you feeling alienated by your friends who are dating? Are you doing your part to keep the friendship alive? Are you allowing jealousy to mess up your friendship? Have you talked to your friend about how you feel? Do you have any suggestions to help the situation? Do you think you might make some of the same mistakes if you were the one in a dating relationship?

I really like the person I'm dating but I feel like the relationship is getting too serious too fast. What should I do?

Talk with him. Let him know you're feeling uncomfortable, but also let him know what you appreciate about the relationship. I was beginning to date a guy my senior year who had gone out with a lot of girls I knew, but he had only taken them out once or twice. We went to a movie and he took my hand. My heart was racing but I was also questioning whether he had any serious feelings for me. I liked holding his hand so I didn't take mine away, but inside I was wondering what would happen next. We had a fun evening that ended in a hug, but I needed to find out where I stood in his eyes. I didn't have the nerve to talk to him so I wrote a letter. I explained that I didn't want him to think of me as old-fashioned, but I needed to know where things were going. He respected my request and slowed down the physical side of our relationship. We've had our struggles, but 2½ years later he still respects me and we are close friends. He still remembers the day I explained my feelings. If a guy really loves you, he will listen to what you say and will want to make you comfortable.

Megan, 19

Try to slow down some. It can usually be done. Sometimes it happens when someone goes away on a vacation, but you can slow it down in other ways too. Watch the activities and things you do together. Try some group dates— some activities with other people. Try writing letters as your mode of communication for a week or two. I did this and it drew me closer to my boyfriend because it allowed me to express some of my feelings in a clearer way. Talk to your friend and let him or her know your thoughts. He may be thinking the same things. Even if he's not, he needs to understand where you're coming from.

Kristin, 18

If you feel your relationship is going too fast, then I would advise you to set limits immediately and tell your friend that things are going too fast. Things can get dangerous if you don't. You might end up forced into something you don't want to do.

Marie, 18

Spend more time with groups of people doing group activities. Also, spend more time in a vertical position rather than a horizontal position. Actually spend more time talking than hugging and kissing.

Adam, 19

Don't do what I did and end the relationship without warning. I didn't even explain the real reason, which was that I felt we were getting too serious too fast. I haven't seen or spoken to that person since. I know I hurt him terribly and I also hurt myself. I do think I should have broken up with him, but I should have been honest and told him why. I learned a hard lesson.

Holly, 19

Communication is the key to any lasting relationship. If this guy really loves you, he will respect your wishes to slow down. Chances are he is having the same feelings as you, or is possibly unaware of your feelings. Just talk to him and be honest. If he doesn't respect your wishes, he is not worth dating.

Anne, 18

Communication is the key. Talk with each other about how you feel. Suggest that you two might back off for awhile and concentrate on the friendship aspect of the relationship. Set limits for yourself on how involved you can get. If you're feeling uncomfortable, let him know. It's okay to take it slower. Take time to build a solid relationship. If you go too fast, it will be flimsy and will eventually crumble.

Joyce, 18

ThiNk AbOuT It

Are you comfortable with how your relationship is progressing? Do you feel it is going to fast? Why? What are you uncomfortable with? What do you want to see change? What do you like? Can you talk with the person you're dating? Do you think communication is vital to your relationship? What should you do in your situation?

The person I'm dating is very possessive and jealous. At first it was kinda neat, but now it's really getting to me. What should I do?

Sure, you thought it was neat in the beginning, probably because it meant he was paying attention to you. But does this mean he really loves and cares for you? No! Being jealous and possessive means you are probably being treated like an object. Yes, it is natural to feel a little jealous sometimes, but the person you are dating seems *too* jealous. I'd talk about it with him. If his attitude doesn't change, I would end the relationship. A good relationship isn't filled with possessiveness and jealousy; it is filled with love and understanding for the other person.

Kim, 18

Let him know how you feel about it. He might really care for you and think this is how you want him to act. It's only fair to communicate. If he's acting this way because he really feels like he owns you, or that you owe him something, then I would get out. A situation like this can only lead to a lot of hurt.

Ellen, 18

I had the same thing happen to me. But, I have to admit, some of it was my fault. I relished the attention and what I perceived as real love and caring. I would become even more devoted if he acted even the least bit jealous. I thought I was cementing our relationship. But I didn't realize how unhealthy it was. I was in counseling because of a very poor self-image. As my self-image improved I began to feel and act more independent. This was a real threat to my boyfriend, and his jealousy and possessiveness intensified as he tried to force me back to the way it had been before. He couldn't accept the new me, even though I was much healthier and could have made him much happier. I finally had to end the relationship. It was really hard, though. He followed me everywhere I went for two months and used to call me at all hours of the night. Finally my dad went and talked to him and his parents. His pursuit stopped, but the memories still hurt. I really encourage you to stop this kind of behavior before it goes any further. Nothing good can come out of it.

Lisa, 19

I was in a relationship with a guy about two years ago who I thought was really awesome. He was the first Christian guy I ever dated. He was also the first guy I ever dated who *really* liked me for me. Everything was too good to be true. I had a guy who really liked me, did everything for me, and was a Christian. Well, for a while it was awesome, but soon it got out of hand. He called me everywhere he went, and surprised me all the time with gifts and flowers. It may seem nice, but I began to feel like I had no room to breathe. Finally I decided to break up with him when I really began to realize how possessive he was of me. He cried like crazy and ended up following me wherever I went and called me all the time. I felt like he was begging me to go back with him. All of this ended up fading, but I was so glad to get out of that relationship. The longer you wait the more you will hurt the guy. Don't stay in a relationship just because you don't want to hurt the other person.

Ami, 18

Jealousy is an evil thing. The tighter a grip jealousy gets on the relationship the more you'll feel crushed. First Corinthians 13 tells us that real love is not jealous but giving and trusting. When your friend is very jealous, he or she will start to dominate and run your life. For true love to happen there *must* be a level of trust.

Michael, 17

If a person is very possessive and jealous, he will eventually become abusive either physically or verbally. In either case, it's wise to get out.

Stephen, 19

Talk about trust. That's the issue. "Do you trust me? If not, why? Have I done anything to show you can't trust me?" I had a boyfriend who was like this. We talked and he opened up a lot. Be willing to listen. There is usually insecurity and pain behind this mistrust. Pray about it. Talk about

it. Put God in the center of your relationship. The growth and
trust that will come is amazing.

Blair, 18

———— ThiNk AbOuT It ————

*What do you think about jealousy and possessive-
ness in a relationship? Is there a part of you that likes
it? Do you think it's part of a healthy relationship?
What would you like your relationship to be like? If
you're wanting more trust, is that something you can
extend to the person you're dating? What do you
think you should do if you're not happy with the
relationship?*

A Further Word...

God wants your dating life to bring you joy.

1 Corinthians 13	Philippians 4:6-8
Matthew 11:28-30	Proverbs 3:5-8
John 14:27	Philippians 4:12,13
Romans 8:28-39	1 John 4:7-12
1 John 5:2-5	Hebrews 4:15,16

chApTer 8

Breaking Up Is Hard to Do

*I dated someone for two years before
breaking up. Will I ever be able to get over him?*   159

*How long should I wait
before I start going out with someone else?*   162

*How can you be in love with
someone one minute, break up with him,
and then not want to have anything to do with him?*   163

*How do I keep from
continuing to be hurt by bad relationships?*   167

I dated someone for two years and then we broke up. I just can't seem to get over him. Will I ever be able to? What should I do?

Well, you will eventually get over him! The first thing you should *not* do is think someone else will help you get over him. Getting involved in another relationship right away will only make things worse. I would say that *time* is the best healer. Take some quality time alone to get to know yourself and come to grips with your feelings. Then you can move on with a pure, natural heart.

Carl, 18

Yes, you will be able to get over him. It may seem hard now, but time can change your perspective on a lot of things. For now it will help you to concentrate on other friendships and realize that your worth and your wholeness as a person don't depend upon that person or his feelings for you.

Angela, 18

I know that breaking up hurts. I went through a relationship of two years and then it ended. She was the girl of my dreams—everything I've ever wanted. For some reason God allowed it to happen. Looking back, I realize that God has always had my best interest at heart. I believe He allowed this in my situation because my relationship with Him was failing. My girlfriend had become number one in my life. Life hasn't been easy since breaking up, but my relationship with God and my dependence on Him has been strengthened.

Mitch, 19

Breaking up is a really difficult thing. It isn't just difficult, it's painful. I guess the first thing I would say is to realize your pain is legitimate. You just lost someone that you care about very much. It's almost like a grieving process. It takes time—lots of time. There is no specific time limit in which you must be over him. Often we put a lot of pressure on ourselves to hurry up and be over hurting. While it's not fun to be in pain, pain is a part of struggling, and struggling is a part of growth. Take time to feel your pain. It's valuable. Don't have pity on yourself, but be understanding of yourself. You've been through a lot, but it will lead to healing. You will get over it in the perfect time.

Marlene, 19

I had gone with the same guy pretty much all through high school. We had always talked about what would happen if we broke up. We said we would always still have feelings for each other—that we would always have a place in our hearts. This year we broke up. I didn't realize how true our thoughts had been; I had so many feelings for him. As time went on, I started to get over him and those feelings got weaker, but he will always have a special place in my heart.

Andrea, 18

This might sound like a really pat answer, but time does ease the heartache. It may take months or even years, but eventually most of the hurt leaves the memories dear to your heart. Sometimes little things will cue you back to your pain—the same "special" look in someone else's eyes, the song that was yours, or a joke you shared—but time does heal. In the meantime, cry and let out what you feel, but don't let yourself be consumed by it. Turn even more to God and rely on Him to help get you through. Maybe talk it out with a parent or a close friend. It's wise to use discretion in talking about it, however. Constantly talking about it may keep your mind on the heartache instead of helping to ease it. Just remember that God is there for you.

Dorothy, 19

Yes, it is possible to get over a person, if you let yourself. You need to let go of the past. Try to focus on other things and other people. Develop new friendships and get involved in new activities. This doesn't mean that you will never think about that person. But don't let the past control your life.

Gretchen, 19

If you truly love the person, healing will take time. It's like death: You love the person and then he leaves your life. You're left with pain and heartache. To be honest, you may always feel a bit of pain and miss the person, but your life can and will go on. I think you should talk with good friends about your hurting. Especially talk and be honest with God. He really cares you know. If you are angry, frustrated, or lonely, tell God and He will take some of the pain on Himself. The healing will take time. There may always be a small part of the pain in your heart, but that's okay. It just means you cared deeply. You will be able to go on and care for someone else deeply again.

Hannah, 19

ThiNk AbOuT It

If you are fresh out of a relationship, what are some activities you can get involved in that you really enjoy? What kinds of things can you pour yourself into? Who are your friends that you can spend quality time with? If you have let those relationships weaken, what can you do to strengthen them? Are you being honest with your feelings? Do you have someone you can talk with? If not, who do you think you would like to talk to?

I've just broken up with someone I've dated for a long time. How long should I wait before I start going out with someone else?

Ever heard of *rebound?* If you start dating right away, all the pain from your previous relationship will be right there and you won't be able to give the new person a fair chance. And that might ruin a possible good relationship. If there is someone waiting in the wings, they'll wait longer if you need the time.

Margo, 18

This totally depends on the individual, but I believe that it is important to be independent for a time after a major breakup. Once you have dealt with your own feelings of hurt and self-image, and you are at peace with God and have prayed about it, then I think it is okay to go out with others.

Lara, 18

Wait long enough to get your feelings straight. If you start dating right away, the feelings you feel may not be real.

It's great to feel appreciated and loved, but you may be confused. I don't think there is any set amount of time. It's a tough call. It's different for everyone.

Anna, 19

That's really a hard question! It totally depends on the person. You need to wait long enough to make sure this new relationship is not taking the place of the old one. Are your feelings straight? Take it slow!

James, 18

There is no set time limit. But it's important that you get over your feelings for the last person. Also, try not to date someone because you miss your ex. I have made this mistake a few times. I found out I just wanted affection, not the person I started dating.

Greg, 19

ThiNk AbOuT It

If you are fresh out of a relationship, what are some things about your last relationship that you would like to see be different in your next one? What would you like to change about yourself? What do you want in your next relationship? What do you not want? What do you want to see happen in yourself before you get involved with someone else?

How can you be in love with someone one minute, break up with him, and then not want to have anything to do with him?

I don't think it was true love. It could be called "extreme like." If you end up not wanting anything to do with him at all, you could have been in love with the *idea* of who you thought he was. When you saw who he really was you didn't like him anymore. Or you could just be in love with the idea of being in love. We all have that problem at least once. Just figure out why you were attracted to someone. If it was mostly looks, next time get to know the person more before you make up your mind. If you are in love with the idea of being in love, then learn patience. God will provide the most wonderful person you could ever have dreamed of. It's not easy, but it has its rewards.

Daphne, 18

I would guess it's more infatuation than love. You probably get too serious too fast, and then you get sick of each other. Friendship first!

Jason, 19

I hate it when people break up and then have nothing to do with each other. If you really care about someone, you need to remain friends. Go out in groups and have fun. It *is* awkward at first, but you have to make an effort. Call the other person and make sure he knows you still care, but are not trying to start things up again. BE REAL! Don't be afraid to tell him you feel awkward. Don't be afraid to tell him you think he is a good friend and that you want to keep the friendship. It may not work in *every* case, but it's a good place to start.

Sally, 19

I think there is something that is difficult for humans to learn and understand, and that is the difference between love and infatuation. In fact, I would venture to say that *most* dating relationships in junior high and high school fall under the category of infatuation. Infatuation tends to focus on temporary, physical, selfish, or shallow things. This is often why there is no attachment after the breakup. Love, on the other hand, is a completely different story. Love involves service and selflessness, and seeks the best for the other person. Love gives someone freedom when he needs it, compassion, and genuineness. In reality, there is much more to love than the "romance" part. I think it's okay if you enjoy dating different people as long as there is an understanding of the difference here. If you find that dating is ruining your friendships in the end, maybe it would be best to stick to forming good foundations for great friendships.

Heather, 19

I think the problem lies in the definition of love. So many times I've seen a guy and instantly fallen "in love" with him. We go out a few times. At the first hitch we break up and never speak again. I've learned that this kind of "love" isn't love at all, but just a strong attraction. Love in the best sense means a commitment. Without a commitment, love won't really happen. I would say the key to breaking the cycle is to step back and look at what love really is. Always be careful not to decide you love someone too quickly. It's so easy to say "I love you" to someone, but when love really isn't there it only hurts when this love is perceived to be lost. Guard your heart.

Caren, 18

I think this question is the story of my life. During junior high and high school, I had a new boyfriend at least every week. I was absolutely sure I was in love. After awhile the guys didn't feel comfortable being in a relationship with me because they could never be sure that my feelings would stay the same. This kind of behavior really hurt a lot of people, as well as hurting myself. Now I realize I was just looking for some sort of security in these guys. Also my relationships turned into really physical things. Slowly I found myself out of my physical boundary zones. Because I thought I loved these people, I let my lustful feelings run my life. I guess what I'm trying to say is if you're not sure about your feelings, or even if you think you know, wait awhile before you let anything happen. It can help you stay out of a lot of trouble.

Tasha, 18

There is a difference between "being in love" with someone and actually loving him. "Being in love" is called infatuation. It can happen in a minute, and end just as quickly. Because it is such an exciting and emotional experience, it's easy to become disappointed when the person turns out to be less perfect than you imagined. Real love takes a long time to develop, and does not happen all at once. You have to be patient, but it's worth the extra effort. True love is forgiving and secure, and will not end suddenly.

Rod, 18

Being "in love" and liking someone are two different things. I thought I was head-over-heels in love with this guy until he really hurt me. Now I realize I didn't "love" him—I just liked him a lot. Love is a very strong word and an even deeper emotion. Take time; don't tell just anyone you love him. Save your love until you know him very well and know he can and will love you back.

Keri, 16

You're not really "in love." This "falling in love" feeling/ attraction is normal, but it is not the same as *love*. To be in love requires that you truly know someone deeply and are deeply attracted to his personality—his very being—regardless of his faults. My point is that relationships are so much deeper than just attraction. Possibly the reason why you are "repulsed" is because you don't really know the person you're dating.

Joanie, 19

ThiNk AbOuT It

Are you afraid to be without a relationship? Why? What are you looking for in relationships? Do you really think you can find what you're looking for that way? What are some other ways you can find what you're looking for? Do you think you can find true security in another person? If not, where can you really find it?

I've broken up with someone three or four times because he treats me so bad, but I keep going back with him. Why am I doing this? How do I keep from continuing to be hurt?

Sometimes the only love a person has ever experienced is bad love. And when your heart really does love someone, whether he is good or bad, it's hard to give up the security of having someone there for you. But no one deserves to be treated badly! You need to start loving yourself and loving God, and realize that God doesn't want you to be hurt or abused. Sometimes it's hard to let go of someone even when he is cruel because you feel it's normal for you to be treated this way. The unknown is scary to people who feel that no one else out there loves them. But think of it this way: Would you want your child to be hurt constantly in an unhealthy relationship? Of course not—so stop the cycle now! Jesus is just like our parents: He doesn't want His children to hurt from a relationship. He wants to be *in* the relationship. Give yourself the respect you deserve and allow God to bless you.

Hope, 19

I was in this situation. I truly believed I loved the person. No matter how bad he treated me I went back to him because I was comfortable with the relationship. I finally got out by spending a *lot* of time praying and by having strong Christian friends who kept me accountable. You can do it!

Katie, 18

I think some people may depend on others, especially the opposite sex, too much. We need to refocus and look at what is good for us and what is bad for us. Do you really need to be in a relationship right now? If you can become more confident, this will help you become stronger so you won't get hurt so deeply. There may still be times when you get hurt, but if God is at the center of your life, you can stay strong.

Mary, 18

I think you may feel like this person is your only option and that no one else will ever like you. Is that why you keep going back to him? This person obviously has no respect for you. Do you respect yourself? Is it possible for you to lose contact with this person? I encourage you to do so. I don't care who you are or where you come from—you deserve to be treated with respect. Don't be scared about being single for awhile. It will be worth it in the end. It will hurt for awhile, but that's better than hurting for a lifetime!

Amy, 19

You are being manipulated. Get counseling or talk with someone you can trust. It's possible that this pattern stems from a prior relationship that hurt you a lot. Maybe it was your parents, an old boyfriend, etc. You deserve to be loved and cherished, but you seem to have been programmed to accept the worst. Sometimes it's hard to change the pattern, but it can be done. Do whatever you have to in order to get help. A lifetime is a very long time to be with someone who hurts you, and life is too short to not make the most of every opportunity and every relationship!

Annie, 19

ThiNk AbOuT It

Examine your past. Are there things there that contribute to the ways you struggle now? Are there things you have never told anyone else? Do you want to talk to someone about them? Is there someone you can trust? Do you want something that happened to you in the past to control your life now? What can you do to stop the cycle?

A Further Word...

Your heart is precious to God.

1 Corinthians 13	Isaiah 53:3-6
James 1:2-5	James 1:12-17
John 10:10	Psalm 16:7-11
Psalm 28:6,7	John 15:9-13
Romans 5:3-8	Proverbs 17:17

chApTer 9

Is This It?

*Is it okay to think
about someone you like all the time?* 173

*How can I know if
I'm in a healthy relationship?* 175

*How do I know if
I'm in love, if it's the real thing?* 178

I really like someone and find myself thinking about him all the time. Is that okay?

I like someone also, and find myself thinking about him too much. I believe it is unhealthy because I often have lustful thoughts which are increasingly hard to push out of my mind. If you truly like the person, think how God would want you to think about him. If you want to achieve a Christ-centered life, you cannot and should not be focused on the person too much.

Betsy, 18

I often wondered the same thing myself. There was this guy I met in a class and we had a lot of fun talking together. We hung out some, but his idea of our relationship and mine were vastly different. I developed a crush on him right away. All I did was think about him and what our relationship was going *to be* like. I thought about everything he said and analyzed it, and debated what it meant. I didn't even realize we were spending less time together, because in my mind we were together, and every syllable he uttered to me in real life confirmed it. I slowly became convinced he liked me. Finally I painfully realized that he *didn't* feel that way about me, but only wanted to be friends.

If you have a good friendship, and are spending time together, you will naturally think about the other person a lot, but don't fool yourself. If you don't know him well, or only say "Hi" in the halls at school, it's not good to think of him all the time. Just let the relationship happen. If you think about that person too much you may put too much pressure on it, have unrealistic expectations, and maybe lose the person as a friend.

Jami, 19

Feelings of attraction for someone are very normal, but try not to be obsessed by thoughts of someone. Learn to think and develop as a person. You can waste a lot of valuable time by focusing on another person only.

Wendi, 17

Of course it's okay! As teens, that's what we do. But it's important to keep our thoughts pure and our eyes on Jesus. Often, thinking about one person only leads to frustration. Ask God for help in maintaining a balance. It could help to ask a Christian friend or leader to hold you accountable in this area.

Hilda, 18

This situation is quite familiar to me in that all too often I build up these wonderful depictions of certain people and glorify them to a ridiculous point. There is nothing wrong with thinking about someone a lot, but the key is *perspective*. Things are never as good as you can make them out to be. Fortunately, God has blessed us with an imagination. Unfortunately, we can get too carried away with our dreams and expectations to the extent that reality is out of focus.

Krissy, 18

Sure! That's perfectly natural! However, remember that your life does need to be well-rounded. Don't forget that your schoolwork, your family, and your friends need your time and love too. Also—and I really struggle with this—when I wake up in the morning my first thoughts are of my boyfriend. My thoughts turn to him often during the day, and I go to sleep dreaming of him at night. The other day it hit me: If I spent half the time thinking about God that I spend thinking about this guy, I'd really be a saint!

Michelle, 18

It's okay to think about the person you like a lot; it's natural. But try to keep life in perspective. It's easy to start fantasizing about a happy life together that will last for eternity. Try to get to know the person on a real level.

Jim, 18

ThiNk AbOuT It

What are the priorities in your life? If you had to list the five most important things in life to you, in the order of importance, what would they be? If you are in a relationship now, do you feel like it rules your life? Is there time and energy for other things?

How can I know if I'm in a healthy relationship? How do I identify and then maintain one?

For the first time in my life I'm in a healthy relationship. I know it because all my past relationships have been centered around physical aspects. It seemed I had to give away part of myself just to keep the relationship. In my present relationship we have decided not to kiss. I don't think there's anything wrong with kissing, but for us it was wrong. We both knew from the start that we liked each other for our hearts, not the physical. We have been going out for six months now and are growing to love each other's hearts more and more every day. We love each other so much that we're not going to let the desires of our flesh destroy the relationship. I don't think kissing always destroys relationships, but it is what follows kissing.

Louise, 18

Healthy relationships are visible because you enjoy each other. You're 100 percent open and honest with each other because you were *friends first!* You love being together, but your main focus is not on the relationship. Give it to God! When He is in control, everything works itself out.

Bonnie, 18

The main indicator of a healthy relationship is honesty—not only with each other, but with yourself as well. When you're being honest about how you really feel about each other, you'll either be willing to work out problems or you won't have the true desire to see situations through to completion.

To maintain a healthy relationship, occasionally question your motivation for doing certain things. Are you focusing on yourself, your friend, or God? A mix favoring the grace of God is the perfect recipe.

Justin, 18

Healthy relationships are found when each person can live independently of each other and still have a happy life. If the relationship is centered in Christ and each person is seeking the Lord's will, as well as purity and holiness for themselves and each other, it should be healthy. If you enjoy each other in good and bad times and complement each other's personalities, it is healthy.

To maintain this, communicate honestly as much as possible. Work through problems and learn to give and take. Keep the relationship centered or focused on the Lord, together and individually.

Barb, 19

I think a healthy relationship consists of two people who have fun together, can laugh together, can be serious with each other, understand each other's feelings, and most of all care about each other. If you're in a healthy relationship you can maintain it by communicating with each other and most of all by being honest with each other. Also, keep your perspective on life clear. Not putting supreme importance on this one relationship can help to keep it healthy.

Kara, 18

A healthy relationship is inclusive. In other words, it makes room for other friendships, new and old. The person you are dating should not become your whole world, because that would be replacing God. He doesn't like that very well, and it just doesn't work out. What would happen if your world were to fall apart? Simply being aware of wanting to be in a healthy relationship is a step in the right direction. Be open to advice from people who already have experience in this area—adults especially. Your parents, as strange as it may seem, are good candidates. It would also most likely be a wonderful relationship builder with them. They want to do whatever they can to help you avoid rough places.

Samantha, 18

What is your definition of a healthy relationship? Do you think you are in one now? Why? What do you think needs to change? Are you willing to do what it takes to make it change? Why?

How do I know if I'm in love? How do I know if the love is the real thing?

This is a really hard question to answer. I think the answer really comes from your own heart, but I'll try my best to answer for you. I was in a lot of relationships before I ever found out what real love was. I thought I was in love a lot of times, but I now realize I was in love with the relationship and not the person. The most important thing is that I had a first love—Jesus. I fell in love with Jesus and then He decided to bless me with a guy. I don't even know if there is such a thing as falling in love. I think you know the love is real when you find joy out of each other's inner selves.

Meredith, 18

One of the best ways to know if you truly love a person is to ask yourself the question, "Do I care more about this person growing closer to Christ, or do I care more about him or her growing closer to me?" If you desire with all your heart for that person to know and trust Christ first, and knowing and trusting you second, then you have true love for someone.

Matt, 19

Can you be completely honest? Can you see the other person's faults and accept him just the way he is? Do you want to give to *him* more than you want him to give to *you?* Can you truly envision yourself spending the rest of your life—another 50 or 60 years—with him? If so, you just might be in love.

Marty, 19

Ask yourself if you care about the other person more than you care about yourself. I think that is true love. It is wanting the best for him, even if it isn't what *you* want. Ask yourself if you love him enough to let him go. *That* is the acid test.

Cameron, 19

Sometimes love will hit you like a lightning bolt, but most times it won't. You have to start with friendship. You need to realize that friendship has to be the foundation of every relationship, and that love grows from there. Otherwise, when you hit those parts of the relationship that are not so attractive, what's left?

Andre, 19

You just can't beat 1 Corinthians 13. Read it and ask yourself if this is how you feel about the person you are considering. If you can't deny yourself for that person's gain, it's not love. Love has a lot to do with being humble, and seeking to understand rather than demanding to be understood. If you're just looking for cuddling, kissing, and smiles, save yourself some time and pain and just rent a movie. Any teen romance movie will do. If you're ready to get off the couch, turn off the TV, and enter into real life, then open your Bible to 1 Corinthians 13, swallow your selfish desires, and go to work.

Jeff, 18

ThiNk AbOuT It

What is your definition of true love? What do you believe are the necessary ingredients? Are you working to become the type of person who will be able to have and give that kind of love? What should you be doing?

A Further Word . . .

God has answers when you don't.

Psalm 27:4,5   Psalm 42:1,2
Psalm 73:23-26   Psalm 84:1,2
Philippians 3:7-12   Colossians 3:1-14

chApTer **10**

I Have This Problem . . .

*I'm 17 and have never been
on a date. Is there something wrong with me?*   183

*The person I'm dating treats a lot
of his friends badly. Should that matter?*   187

*My girlfriend cheated on me.
Should I forgive her and keep dating her?*   189

My boyfriend is my whole world. Is that a problem?   190

My best friend and I both like the same guy. Help!   193

*Is is possible to make
a long-distance relationship work?*   195

Is it okay to date someone of a different race?   198

*My boyfriend gets upset when I
talk to other guys. What should I do?*   201

*The person I'm dating and I
fight a lot. Should I stay in this relationship?*   205

What should I do if my boyfriend hits me?   207

*Do I need to tell the person
I'm dating about mistakes I've made in the past?*   212

I'm 17 and have never been on a date. I don't think I'm ugly. Is there something wrong with me?

I'm 19 and I didn't go out on a date until quite recently. I'm a popular, well-liked person. Often God keeps us from dating to spare us, though it never feels like that at the time. I've survived 19 years of a dateless life quite happily. I've been quite content, even though it's not always easy to be "dateless." I think my solution was to throw myself into the life God has given me—friends, choir, theater, youth group—trusting that God would bring dates into the life I was living. The alternative is just waiting around, always looking out for a date. In short, my answer is the tried and true "Let go and let God."

Karla, 19

Nothing is wrong with you! I was the same way. The guys I liked never liked me and the guys I didn't like flocked to me! I formed some nice friendships, but I didn't get into a relationship until I started college. I always ended up going to prom, dances, etc. with close guy friends and I had a blast. The important thing is to trust in God and don't feel you have to be dating.

Mollie, 19

There is definitely nothing wrong with you. I have this belief that right now God is preparing me for someone and preparing that person as well. When the time is right we will be together. Try to realize that God is preparing you for something good.

Allen, 19

I'm almost 19 and have never been on a date. I've tried to look at myself objectively (on the inside, not the outside) to see if there was anything that might need to be changed. I'm not talking about pretending to be a different person, but becoming a better one. From looking at myself, and getting some honest input from friends, I discovered I could be rather intimidating to others. I didn't think I was, but now I've been working on seeming more approachable. Another thing is the fact that I believe God must have some purpose behind this—what, I don't know. Maybe God knows that somehow I'm just not ready. Still, I trust in God and do have hope, since 90 percent of the population does eventually get married!

Sue, 18

Okay, let's be honest. I'm not what you would consider a pretty girl, but I'm not down on myself. I've just accepted the fact that by the world's standards I am not especially attractive. When I was younger I was really depressed by this, so I quit caring about myself. In addition to not being very attractive, I was overweight, my hairstyle was awful, my clothes were shapeless bags, and I didn't work at staying all that clean. What difference did it make anyway? Gradually a close adult friend helped me realize I really did have worth as a person. I decided to work on what I could do something about. I lost a lot of weight by going on a regular exercise plan and eating right. Once I had lost the weight I got a good haircut, and my folks bought me some new clothes. And I definitely took good care of myself. As I worked on being all I could, my self-confidence grew and I became more out-going. My basic looks hadn't changed but my insides had! I made a lot of new friends and got involved in a lot of activities. My senior year I even started dating a guy. I know he loves me for who I am, because it's sure not my looks! My point is that you may not be ugly, but are you being all you can be? Are there things about yourself you need to change? If there are, then be honest enough to admit it. Then do what it takes to change it. You might be surprised at the results.

Jill, 18

I was just like you! No, there is nothing wrong with you. Patience really does pay off. I seriously believe God sent me my first boyfriend my senior year of high school. He was so good to me and treated me so well. When all my friends had been on so many dates that had been terrible, I wasn't having the same experience and couldn't relate. So don't worry. You certainly aren't alone. You have been spared a lot of heartache. I no longer go out with that guy, but he was worth waiting for. I really believe God gives us the desires of our hearts—in His time! Pray for patience and peace; it helped me a lot!

Tori, 19

People tell me just to wait and it will come. But let's be realistic—there are more Christian girls than Christian guys out there. I know some really incredible women who have never married. There is definitely nothing wrong with them. It's just that at this point God hasn't brought the right man into their lives. Some of them are in their thirties and forties. Face it—it may not be God's will for you to be married. Having a lot of older women friends has helped me think about this. I can't just wait around for "Mr. Right." I have to make the most of my life the way it is. I have vowed to make the most of every day, to become all that God has for me. If "Mr. Right" comes along, great! If not, I'll still be okay. I'm still precious to God and I'll have even more time to give to people and make a difference in this world. Marriage and being in love is not all there is!

Monica, 19

I went on my first date at 18 in my freshman year of college. Talk about dull, painful teen years! I remember going to homecoming my senior year, not to dance or date like everyone else, but to announce the court. Oh, the humiliation! I can remember thinking throughout high school that I would do anything for a date! Yet I'm so thankful that God spared me by preventing me from dating. Perhaps I can be a little more clear: I was shy, studious, and slightly overweight. I would develop crushes on unattainable, nonthreatening guys whom I never expected to meet. Eventually I despised myself so deeply that I starved myself to no more than a skeleton. Only the threat of a hospital stay for psychological instability, two years of counseling, and most of all the grace of a very merciful God spared me.

Now I have Matthew. We are going on our sixth month and have spent massive amounts of time together—staying for two weeks at each other's houses over Christmas, touring together with an acting group, studying, praying, walking, and just being. He is my best friend, my playmate, my partner in discussion, and my brother in Christ. He loves me for who I am—I don't need to try and be anything else.

Wait on God! In the right time he will bring someone into your life. I will always pay for my anorexia. I may never have children and may never be able to express my love for Matt in that way. I am still too thin, but I cannot *want* to be heavier. Love is not just warm fuzzies. It costs, and it hurts, but it should *never* ask you to be something you are not.

Concentrate on being who God wants you to be, and you'll find that His timing and His will for you are perfect!

Patricia, 19

ThiNk AbOuT It

Do you think there is a certain time when you should begin dating? Do you believe you have less value if you don't have a boyfriend or girlfriend? Are you doing all you can to become everything you should be? Are there things you need to focus on in your own life before you start dating?

The person I'm dating treats me really well, but treats a lot of his friends badly. Should that matter?

I think it should matter, but each person must decide. I actually broke up with a boyfriend because he had changed from the kind and caring guy I started dating to one who started ignoring others—except me. This got on my nerves so I tried to talk with him, but he didn't really seem to make an effort, so I decided to end the relationship.

Brenda, 18

The person I date has to be my friend. If the person you are dating is capable of treating his friends badly, is he capable of treating *you* badly? I think this matters, and maybe you should look a little closer and see if he is really treating you well. Realize that his behavior could extend to you at any time.

Allison, 18

YES! The way people treat their friends and family is a direct reflection of how they could very possibly treat you after the initial lovey-dovey stuff wears off.

Hollymarie, 17

Yes, it matters. Although it's great that he treats you well, the way he treats others reflects his heart. I wouldn't want to get involved with a guy who loves inconsistently.

Nicki, 19

Yes, it should matter because now he has to be on his best behavior with you, because if he's not he knows he may lose you. But the way he treats his friends could be a good indication of how he will treat you if you marry him because then he's "got you."

Andy, 18

This matters a lot. How people act toward their friends is a reflection of their true selves. It is possible to see the real person when he's around the people he's most comfortable with. He may treat you well right now, but look out later on when he feels secure enough with you to be natural.

Ned, 18

ThiNk AbOuT It

What are the best ways to judge someone's character? Do you think how he or she treats others is important? How he treats his friends? How he treats his family? How he treats strangers? How do you rank in these categories? What can people tell about your character by how you act? Are there things you think you should change?

I'm dating someone on a steady basis. She just told me she had gone out with someone else but promised to never do it again. Should I forgive her and keep dating her?

Good question. Why did she go out with someone else? Obviously trust will not be the same for awhile, but if you think you love her, you must give her time to earn the trust back.

Dave, 19

If she has given you no other reason in the past to doubt her, then definitely forgive her and continue dating her. But make sure she knows she can't keep letting you down and expect you to keep running back.

Caitlin, 16

Yes, you can forgive her, but maybe you should discuss what your commitment is. You don't need to have a strictly exclusive relationship unless you are engaged. Physically, if you are seriously dating someone, it is probably not a good idea to go around kissing everyone you date. But a certain freedom is necessary to keep it healthy. If you really like each other you can afford to take other people out and have a good time.

Janice, 19

Ultimately, you have to decide. But keep in mind that you're not married and there was no adultery here. True, a trust could be broken, but don't take these things too seriously. They're only human, after all.

Gerri, 18

ThiNk AbOuT It

Are you able to honestly communicate mistakes that you make in your relationships? Do people feel free to honestly communicate with you? Do you consider yourself to be a forgiving person? What things are you willing to compromise on in a relationship? What things will you stand firm on?

My boyfriend and I broke up but got back together after a week. It really scared me, though, because I felt like my whole world had fallen apart. I'm not sure that's good. What do you think?

I know it's easy to think about someone all the time, but you can be happy and complete without him. He should not be your whole world. You should realize that you have worth just because you *are*, and not because you're involved with someone else.

Stacey, 18

I had the same thing happen to me. I was surprised at how devastated I was. I didn't realize how much I had come to depend on him. I talked about it with some friends and realized I needed to have a life of my own. We got back together, but it wasn't the same again. I developed a life away from him and encouraged him to do the same. We have a much better relationship now because we both have different things to bring to it. I'm glad we broke up, because I probably would have gone on that way for a long time and then been really sorry about how much I had missed out on.

Lisa, 18

I think it's important to take time. I've been through the same situation before and I really don't think one week is long enough. You need time to sort out and deal with your emotions. I know it's hard and it hurts like crazy! I remember feeling like my heart was breaking in two and I think I flooded my house with tears. It's tempting to get back together, but this is a time when you can really lean on God, family, and friends for support. Pray for God's will. If He wants you back together, He will lead you together. It's also important for you to find out why you can't be happy without him. That doesn't sound healthy. He should only add to the happiness in your life that is already there.

Ginger, 18

I broke up with my boyfriend and discovered the same thing: He was my whole life. But the time we spent apart made me learn some things. You need to be a stronger, more independent person. Don't rely on him. Get involved in more activities. Spend more time with friends. You'll be much happier and your relationships will be healthier.

Virginia, 18

My boyfriend was beginning to be my whole world. Because of this we decided we needed time to be apart and reprioritize our lives. God should be first in any romantic relationship you have. When both you and another person are committed to God first, and then each other, somehow it just seems to bring you closer. Right before we "separated," we prayed together. Not only did we pray for us, but we also prayed for family, for friends, and for God's will to be done. I have never felt closer to my boyfriend than in that time we spent talking together with God. I want that kind of close- ness with someone in the future, be it my boyfriend now or someone else. I am willing to endure separation now in order to have that type of relationship in the future.

Carlene, 19

Feeling as if he's your whole world is wrong. If you are a Christian, no one should rank higher than God. And no matter who you are, you shouldn't value your friend more than you value yourself. If you need him to feel good, then maybe you should look at your life and figure out why you are dating him. Is it because you like him, or because you like feeling special enough to have a boyfriend? Having a boyfriend makes you no more or less valuable a person than not having one. God loves us all the same.

Nicole, 19

The problem with this relationship is that the focus is wrong. Your friend should not be your whole world. No relationship is complete without being centered on Christ. A relationship should not be only between two people, but also with Christ—sort of a triangular relationship. By focusing on God, you will grow together in all ways. There will not be a gaping hole if the relationship ends; rather, Christ will be there.

Brad, 18

ThiNk AbOuT It

Where do you find your value? Do you believe you're a whole person even if you lose the person you are currently dating? Who is number one in your life? Do you think that is the best formula for you to be happy? Do you consider yourself an independent, strong person? Why? Where does God fit into the picture of your relationships?

My best friend and I both like the same guy. I think he likes me best, but I don't want to lose my best friend. What should I do?

Your best friend will probably still be around when the potential boyfriend disappears. Do as you would have her do unto you.

Julie, 18

Since you and your best friend get along so well and have similar interests, it's totally natural for you to like the same guy. The same situation happened to me with my best friend and one of our good friends. She asked him to the prom. We ended up double-dating and I flirted with him the whole night. My best friend was really mad. The next day we fought, and then realized how important our friendship really was to us. We decided that our friendship had endured too much to let one boy come between us. Now she is still my best friend who I love very much and we both still have a wonderful friendship with our guy friend.

Celeste, 19

I have had the exact same thought. I decided to put my friendship first and try to forget the guy. I'm so glad I did. The guy turned out to be not interested in either of us and we've been best friends for the last five years.

Pamela, 19

This is a tough situation, but the best thing to do is to let your friend know that you like him too. Admit that you don't want to hurt them, but you don't need to voice speculations that may or may not be true. If he asks one of you out, your questions will be answered. If you have talked about it before, it won't seem like you went about it underhandedly.

Teresa, 19

I've been in this situation before. I would advise against going out with this guy or even considering dating him. There will always be another guy that will come along. It's not worth losing your best friend. I would talk to her about it. Ask her how she feels and what she would think if you got together with this person.

Sandra, 18

I think you should figure out which is more important— your best friend and her feelings or a relationship. Your friend may say she doesn't mind if you begin to date this person, but because we are human, those feelings of envy and strife will keep coming up.

Johnny, 19

Don't ever allow a person to come between a friendship! Guys and gals come and go quickly. In the meantime you will have lost your best friend.

Violet, 19

ThiNk AbOuT It

What would you do if you and your best friend liked the same person? Could you talk about it? What would you say? What would you want him or her to do for you? Which relationship do you think is more important?

The person I'm dating has gone off to college. Is it possible to make a long-distance relationship work?

Long-distance relationships are very hard. I am presently in a relationship with a woman I love with all my heart. We are separated by 1650 miles. But if you are really in love, it will work. Phone bills are high, but I say it's worth it. I have found that my love has grown for her since I can't see her every weekend. I really love her for who she is and not because she is incredibly beautiful. *You* cannot make the relationship work. Just let it flow along, and through prayer, let God direct it.

Joseph, 19

I was in this exact same situation a year ago. It *is* possible to make a long-distance relationship work. My relationship now is evidence of it. Here is how we kept the relationship alive: LETTERS—lots of letters. You'd be surprised how good letters are for the relationship. First, deep and interesting things come out on paper. Second, they help to develop patience. *Not only plain old letters, but creative care packages.* I once sent him a package containing 12 individually wrapped letters with instructions to open one each hour of the day. The letters included notes of encouragement and memories of our relationship. Phone calls, visits, and prayer are the other things that kept our relationship alive.

Paula, 18

A long-distance relationship is a learning tool. There are nearly as many frustrations as there are benefits: less physical temptation; increase in value of time; appreciation of voice by phone and of mind by mail; a sure indication of whether both persons will serve from their heart or not; and a large amount of room for God to work and lead. Perhaps in the process of kindling a long-distance relationship God will demonstrate that the best part of dating is not making out, but holding a friend's heart with care even when he or she is not there. Integrity is sharpened in times like this.

Anthony, 19

Long-distance relationships are incredibly hard and often don't work. But if you are willing to work at your relationship, it is possible to have a successful one. Both of you must be committed to making it work. Close or apart, you can spend time in writing letters or talking on the phone. I would strongly encourage letter writing as it is easier on the pocketbook. Also, it is often easier to communicate your deeper thoughts and feelings by letter rather than over a quick (or long) phone conversation. In a long-distance relationship you must open up more quickly and deeply when you have the chance because you don't have as much time together. I encourage praying together over the phone, because prayer will bond you two and will help you share more intimately than you might otherwise. Keep each other in prayer often. In fact, I think prayer is the single most important factor in surviving a long-distance relationship.

Along with that, communicate, communicate, communicate! Share emotions, everyday things, thoughts, and opinions. Don't mope around. It's okay to be sad, but it's not okay to mope. When you feel particularly lonely, seek out someone whom you can minister to or encourage. Tell God about your loneliness. Even more than that, praise Him for what He has done in your life. Praise Him for the way your hurt is making you into pure gold. That will ease your pain. I know, for I have done it. You will still miss that special someone, but it will be easier if you praise God and seek to encourage others. You will also need to allow the other person freedom to make friends with members of the opposite sex when he or she is away from you. If your relationship is meant to be, this will strengthen it as you each realize more and more what you appreciate about the other.

Esther, 19

If you are not up to a big challenge and a lot of self-sacrifice, then don't attempt a long-distance relationship. The biggest key to survival is making the relationship a 24-hour-a-day one in spite of the distance. To me this meant writing my girlfriend every day, even if it was just a postcard that said "Hi." The phone is another obstacle. You will be faced with financial obstacles, so be smart; don't try to wrestle out a huge fight on the phone. Oftentimes, three hours and 25 dollars later, you are none the wiser and definitely poorer. Instead, decide to get off the phone and write a letter. It took me a couple of 200-dollar phone bills to learn this lesson.

Long-distance relationships are great for testing intentions. A relationship rooted in physical gratification will quickly fall apart. Why? If you're looking for physical satisfaction you can find a lot of girls who fit the order right at your location. However, if the relationship is built on a real foundation of respect and love for a special person, then no one will come between that if you're smart. By smart I mean *protect what's valuable.* Don't be paranoid, but also don't be careless in your relating to the opposite sex. The desires of our heart are not always good, and temptation and lust like to distort our judgment. I've loved being able to focus on friendships with guys that I didn't have in high school because I was always chasing girls. I now have some great male friendships and a girlfriend that I love and respect for being a beautiful person. The struggles of distance and God's grace made that possible.

Jerrod, 18

ThiNk AbOuT It

Do you think a long-distance relationship is worth the pain and struggle? Do you think you have what it takes to make it work? Does the other person? What do you think will be your biggest obstacles? How can you overcome them?

I really like this guy but we are not the same race. Should that matter? Is it okay to date someone of a different race?

God created us all in His image. Dating someone of a different race would be no worse than a short person dating a tall person. Love is blind!

Eddie, 18

I'm Chinese and I don't think I've ever dated a Chinese person (well, maybe one!). I think it's okay to date a person of a different race. The *last* thing that should affect a relationship is race. There are a few things to be aware of, though. First, a relationship is built mainly on personalities and less on looks and skin color (though it is hard to not notice these aspects). Second, a relationship built between races may also have cultural differences. For the other person to understand where you may be coming from in an argument or situation, he or she may need to know more about your cultural background. Third, if the relationship is a serious one, don't forget about your parents. When I dated an Indian fellow, my parents became kind of concerned for many reasons. The biggest problem my parents had with my boyfriend was their relationship with *his* parents. As much as the relationship is yours, do remember your parents. They care about you and they would definitely want you to be happy in a lifelong relationship.

Nancy, 18

Race should not matter, and I believe that biblically there is nothing wrong with it. But you need to make sure that you personally are ready to handle the pressures of interracial dating. Unfortunately, in the United States interracial dating can be very difficult and stressful. You need to be sure you are confident and strong enough within yourself to handle the pressure of a dating relationship along with the added pressure of racism.

Laura, 19

I believe it is wonderful if you can find someone who you really love, no matter what race he or she is. I would warn you, though, that this type of dating relationship brings extra problems with it. My first boyfriend was an Indian and it would sometimes feel awkward just to walk down the street with him because of all the people who stared at us. Also, keep in mind that he or she could have been raised in a very different way than you have.

Rhonda, 19

I've dated three people who are not of the same race as I am and I have had wonderful relationships with all of them. I see nothing at all wrong with interracial relationships if the two people involved are able to handle it. People are people no matter what their race, creed, heritage, or background.

Everyone has something to offer, so don't cheat yourself, and another person, out of a possibly fulfilling relationship simply because of the fact that you aren't the same race.

Amy, 18

My father is Black and my mother is Hispanic. They have a wonderful relationship! I hope my own marriage will be like theirs one day. A lot of the family had a hard time with their marriage at first, but over the years it has gotten better. They have been married for almost 20 years and their love for each other is incredible. They admit there have been struggles but they would do it all over again if they had the choice! There have been times when I have struggled with being a mixed-race person, not because of the way I view it, but because of the way others view it. But it has made me stronger and I know more about myself. I like who I am and I wouldn't want to be any different. I love both of my parents and I'm glad I have a part of both of them in me!

Connie, 18

I am Caucasian and my boyfriend is Oriental. We have a wonderful relationship, and we love each other for who we are on the inside, not the outside. This does not mean that the relationship is easy, however. There are many aspects of cross-cultural relationships that must be dealt with. For example, I don't speak his native language, so conversation with his parents is fairly difficult. I don't know how to cook the food he likes. We have different traditions, customs, and ideas. My parents are fairly conservative, so they are struggling with accepting the relationship. So many things will have to be confronted and dealt with. But with love, patience, and honesty, it is possible to have a fulfilling relationship. My boyfriend and I are careful to respect the cultural norms of each other's family and we try to meet each other halfway concerning difficult issues. Communication and openness are keys in cross-cultural relationships. It takes hard work, but you may just find the love of your life!

Joy, 19

I have a very good friend who is of a different race and we've talked a lot about this kind of stuff. It shouldn't matter to you, but if you get really serious (as in marriage), you have to consider that when you marry someone, you also marry a family. That family may have very different customs, attitudes, and mannerisms than you. Also, you must consider the feelings of your families. Their approval is very important. Finally, you must consider racism. Interracial couples are not always looked upon in the best light, and you should consider your children. Some interracial children have great difficulty in finding a place to belong. They can be shunned by both races. I once knew a girl who was half African-American and half Caucasian. She was viewed as a Black by Caucasians, but by the Blacks she was persecuted as a dishonor to the race. She didn't belong anywhere. It can be really hard.

Katrina, 18

ThiNk AbOuT It

Is race difference important to you? Do you consider yourself prejudiced or open-minded? Do your actions and thoughts support your beliefs? How do you think your parents would respond to an interracial relationship? Have you thought through all the possible consequences of your relationship?

My boyfriend gets upset when I just talk to other guys. It's not like I'm looking for

another relationship. I just want to be friends. What should I do?

I had this problem, but I didn't realize it at first. Once I found out that my girlfriend was really hurt and jealous about this, it kind of shocked me. For awhile after the confrontation I was scared just to say "Boo" to another girl. It shouldn't be that way, however, at least at the beginning of a relationship. You need to both have an understanding that, based upon previous relationships (not the "dating" kind), your friend may have really good and nurturing friendships with members of the opposite sex. To ask him or her to give up these other relationships would be a very selfish and self-centered expectation.

Kyle, 19

This question hit me because I've been going through the exact same problem. First, try to put yourself in his position; a lot of guys are possessive. Second, confront him. Is this something he is willing to work on? Does he trust you? He may just need to feel that he is adequate enough for you. If his attitude bothers you and it doesn't change, then you need to ask yourself if you can handle his possessiveness. It could get worse if he's not willing to deal with it.

Heather, 18

It sounds like your friend doesn't feel very secure in your relationship. I have a friend who has been dating one guy for several years. This guy becomes very angry whenever she talks to other guys or he thinks guys are looking at her "the wrong way." This has caused her to alienate herself from her friends because she feels her relationship to her boyfriend should come first. It's not your fault that you want to be friends with members of the opposite sex. It's perfectly natural and normal. Remember, you're single until you're married. No one owns you or your time completely, or has any right to. Even when married, there needs to be trust to allow you to have friendships with other people. Think hard about this relationship. Is it really what you want? Are you really happy like this? What is best for you?

Mandy, 18

Try to let him or her know how you feel and that you want to maintain friendships with people of the opposite sex. If he insists that you stay away from the opposite sex, then maybe you should reconsider your relationship. Be careful: Possessive behavior and jealousy are two warning signs of an unhealthy dating relationship.

Ben, 19

Explain to your friend that in order for this relationship to work he has to accept (not like or enjoy necessarily, but accept) your friendships. If he can't accept your friends then you can't live your life and he isn't worth it!

Dee, 16

The same thing happened to me, but I made a big mistake. In order to hold on to my boyfriend, I ended my friendships with all other male friends, and most of my girlfriends. I was so insecure that I was willing to do anything to hold onto my boyfriend. At first I thought it was neat that he cared that much. I found out, though, that one person can never meet *all* your needs. I needed and wanted my other friends. After a year my boyfriend broke up with me and I found myself with no friends. It was so hard! I had to start all over again. I will never make the same mistake again. If your friend really loves you he will want you to have a well-rounded life with a lot of good friends.

Ashley, 19

Evaluate the relationship and yourself:
1) Is your boyfriend insecure about himself and therefore paranoid that you will run off with someone else?
2) Are you just "talking" to other guys, or is your body language showing something else?
3) Why are you talking to the other guys? To be friends? To be impressive? To make your own boyfriend pay more attention?

Check your motives and make sure your heart and attitude are pure. If you feel confident they are, then you must settle this with your boyfriend because in the end it will destroy your relationship. It is healthy to have lots of friends of both sexes and no one has the right to dictate whether or not you can have them.

Brittany, 18

I have had this problem myself, and what I've learned is that you both have to work on it. I would examine your "talking." I used to flirt like crazy in front of my guy. It was neither nice nor smart. Be courteous. Try to devote time to him if you truly care about him. If you do this, and talk to him about it, hopefully he'll calm down. If not, maybe he sees you more as property than as a person. I'd be really careful.

Ann, 18

ThiNk AbOuT It

Do you have friends of both sexes? Do you look at people of the opposite sex as friends, or are they just dating possibilities? Do you (or would you) give your boyfriend or girlfriend freedom to develop friendships with both sexes? Why?

My boyfriend and I fight a lot, but when we're not fighting we have a good time. Should I stay in this relationship?

Do the good aspects outweigh the bad aspects? If there is more bad than good, MOVE ON! God won't leave you on your own. Since fighting does not constitute loving, I might see this as a problem. If this is a regular occurrence, there might be bigger problems you might have to deal with. Life is too short and love is too obvious to misread. Deep in your heart, with God's loving guidance, I believe you know the answer.

Kitty, 19

I've always been told that your relationship can't be healthy if you never fight. I think that if you do fight, but are able to talk things out and go on, you should stay in the relationship. But if you fight about the same thing over and over again and it never seems to be resolved—if no one is trying to change—then you're probably never going to be fully happy in that relationship.

Susan, 18

I feel it is wise for you to get out of the relationship and just be friends. Some people are more compatible as just

---

daTing

friends. Backing off and deciding to just be friends could mean that you have a long, satisfying friendship instead of becoming bitter and resentful toward each other.

Lindsey, 18

My girlfriend and I are very different in many aspects. We are both Christians but we used to fight a lot until we became very honest with each other and realized that we aren't going to be identical in everything. We decided that with strong communication we could work through a lot of our differences. Now we rarely fight, and we have been together for several years. Whenever we do have an argument, I try my hardest to value her feelings above mine and to think of how I would react if I were in her shoes.

Brent, 19

It depends on whether the fighting is physical or verbal. If it's verbal, is it abusive, or just arguing? Fighting can sometimes be a healthy part of a relationship. You will not always see eye to eye on every issue. The way you fight, though, is important. I don't think it's ever okay to yell and scream at each other. You can argue about something and still be civilized. You need to be able to respect the other person even when you are disagreeing. If that is not happening, and things don't change, I think the relationship will only hurt you.

Ryan, 19

I think you need some time apart to get your focus straight. Spend time alone praying. Get God in the center of your lives, then pray TOGETHER to put God in the center of your relationship. Ask God to teach you how to love each other. If there is no change, you need to get out.

Ardith, 18

My parents have that kind of relationship. When they're not fighting, they seem to have a good time. The problem is that they spend almost all their time fighting. It's gotten worse with time. I know one thing: I don't want to have a relationship like that! The good times are not worth the pain of the fighting. If I can't resolve differences with someone without fighting, then I'll be alone until God provides me with the right person for me.

Johnsie, 18

ThiNk AbOuT It

How necessary is conflict in a relationship? Do you think it's healthy? Why? What do you think is the best way to handle differences? Do you have the ability to communicate about the things that are important to you? Is this something you want to work on? How can you do that?

My boyfriend hit me the other day and really scared me. He was sorry and promised it would never happen again. What should I do?

Imagine doing the most sinful thing you could possibly ever do. Then imagine standing in front of Jesus. Would He hit you? No way! He would forgive you and love you all the more for it. So what gives your boyfriend the right to hit you when you did absolutely nothing to deserve it? Nobody deserves to be hit. And no one has the right to abuse his girlfriend that way. And think about this: If he's hit you once already, what's going to stop him from doing it again, especially if he knows you will forgive him every time? I think you should get *out* of the relationship. Don't become another statistic. You're worth more than that!

Jennifer, 18

No matter how sorry he was, he should never have done it. If he respects you and truly loves you, he will not have the strength to raise a hand against you. You are worth a lot more and deserve more than him.

Tara, 18

I have played football for the last eight years and have delivered my share of violent blows. I've also received my share of them. Guys seem to be surrounded with violent feelings and even are sometimes expected to act violently. Is this an excuse for hitting a girl? NO WAY! Our society may think it is cooler to hit a girl than to cry, but our society is sick! I believe in the forgiveness brought by the blood of Christ, but if violence persists, either physically or emotionally, get away fast. If your boyfriend has hit you there is only one appropriate response on his part: "I'm sorry." There is no reason good enough for a man to be justified in hitting a girl. Nothing you do deserves a violent response. NOTHING!

Brandon, 18

Two years ago I was dating a respectable, popular, intelligent, good-looking guy. From a distance he would seem like a girl's dream man. For the first part of our relationship he was my "knight in shining armor." He treated me like a princess and made me feel special. He told me he loved me. I believed him. I thought I loved him, too.

About three months into our relationship things began to change. He became very possessive and jealous. We never went out in groups unless we were with his friends. He would often provoke me to anger, and eventually to tears.

I Have This Problem...

Some dates were so bad that I became physically ill. My stomach would tighten up in knots because of the way he treated me. We continued to fight more and more. Each time he became more and more aggressive. He was a brilliant talker and knew exactly what to say to "push my buttons." At first I fought back, but eventually it got so bad I would just break down into tears. He intimidated me so much that I lost all power to communicate. One night as we were coming home from the movies, we had the worst fight ever. He started to criticize me and my involvement in theater. We had several fights over my shows because he hated the amount of time they took. I lost it and really let him have it verbally. I could tell he was really angry and I was scared.

I will never forget the look in his eyes when he hit me. His fist was hard and my face burned with the pain. I was in shock. I tried to scream, but I had no voice. He grabbed me and pinned me down on the seat of the car. He hit me three more times across the face, and then he let me go. It was at that moment that he realized what he had done, but it was too late. He shook with fear and began to cry. I was crying already. He pulled me close and repeatedly apologized. I felt so sick. I just wanted to die. I didn't know what to do. After about ten minutes he acted like everything was fine. He started kissing me and trying to touch me. He told me he wanted to make love to me—that it would make it all better. That is the last thing I wanted to do, but I was so scared I didn't dare challenge him. I have never felt so degraded and cheap in my whole life!

I'm ashamed to say that this pattern continued for about a year before our relationship ended. I was caught in a deadly trap and there seemed to be no escape. I had such a low self-image that I honestly believed I deserved exactly the punishment I got. After all, he was the kind of guy that most girls dreamed about. I didn't think anyone would believe me, so I never said a word, not even when confronted by family and friends.

I got away from the relationship when I came to college. He did his best to control me, but because of the distance between us, I was free from his iron fist. I began to grow my own wings. Slowly I began to realize the horror of the relationship. At this point God began to really work in my life. He restored my self-image and filled me with a new peace. He gave me strength to stand up for myself.

It has taken me awhile to be able to trust a man again, but this past summer God brought someone very special into my life. He is a Christian and I am proud and excited to say that we have a wonderfully healthy relationship. This new relationship is nothing like the last one. For the first time I am happy—really happy. I am not scared, angry, or emotionally or physically threatened. God is the center of the relationship and it's the best ever!

If you are in a destructive relationship, or ever find yourself in a physically threatened position, tell someone! No one deserves to be physically abused or emotionally destroyed. It isn't easy, but you must stand up for yourself. You are a valuable human being and you deserve to be treated with respect. Don't settle for second best simply because you are afraid that no one else will like you. It is better to be single than to be with the wrong person. I only wish someone had told me that fact before I had to learn it the hard way. One thing is for sure: No one will ever hit me again and get away with it!

Melanie, 19

My heart reaches out to you in love and urges you to get out of the relationship! There is no excuse for physical or verbal abuse. It's very, very wrong. Draw close to God, your friends, and your family.

Melissa, 19

Get away as fast as you can. Several of my friends got in that situation. None of the guys improved; they only built on their past behavior to take even more control of the situation. You are under no obligation to stay with him, or even talk to him if he continues. His problem is *not* yours. Don't think your actions will cure him in any way. Hitting you is just one sign of a much deeper problem the guy has with women and you *can't help!* Get away!

Leslie, 19

I've had several friends in abusive relationships. GET OUT! I don't care how much you think you love him. Get out immediately. The person can prove that he is different, and has changed, by getting help or something, but you need to set a big distance between the two of you.

Debra, 18

When people abuse you they are very likely to repeat it. Even if they are sorry and don't do it again, the scars will remain with you. Don't feel you need to erase these hurts just to soothe someone else's conscience. Forgive, yes. But don't place yourself in the situation again.

Debbie, 18

If he hit you once, it is easier for him to hit you again. When you look for a mate, you want someone with whom you feel safe. He should want the best for you and love you enough to want to protect you—not hurt you.

Bea, 19

_____ ThiNk AbOuT It _____

Do you believe you deserve to be valued and re-
spected as a special person? Why? How do you
expect other people to treat you? If you had a friend
who was being abused, what should you do? What
would be the best way to show love to this person? If
you're being abused, do you really want to continue
living this way? What can you do to get help? What
are you waiting for?

I've made some mistakes in the past. Should I tell the person I'm dating about them?

Communication is a must in a relationship. Without that, many relationships break up. If it crossed your mind about telling him, then that means you think you should. Therefore, don't be afraid—tell him. If he isn't willing to accept you for who you were in the *past* and who you are *now*, then maybe you shouldn't even be involved with him. Understanding is another major *must* in a relationship.

Corrie, 18

Only tell him if he means a lot to you and it is a pretty serious relationship. Other than that, everybody makes mistakes, so don't feel obliged to tell him about your past because he might not deserve to know.

Stacy, 18

I don't think he needs to know every detail, but I don't think it's necessary, or fair, to keep secrets either, especially if your mistakes could affect the person you're presently dating.

Joyce, 18

I don't think you need to spill your guts on the first date, but it is important to communicate with the one you are dating. I believe as a relationship progresses and the couple begins to know each other better, they can reveal more of their past lives. If the individual you are dating has such a problem with your past that he sees fit to break up with you over it, then he was not the right one for you in the first place.

George, 19

Tell him, but not all at once. You don't want to dump everything at once on him. Tell bits in stages and allow him time to deal with what you've told him. And be very open and forgiving when he tells you about his own past. Chances are he isn't perfect either.

Mani, 19

Only if the person wants to know. Don't tell the person out of feelings of guilt. Only share if you are comfortable. Some things need to stay in the past. Respect the person, though. If you think your past mistakes could really affect how that person feels, then you need to be honest. Never lie! Good relationships are built on trust.

Lavonne, 18

I really don't think you have to share all the mistakes of your past unless you think it is important for him to know. If you feel like you're hiding something from him, or feel like you're being dishonest, then maybe you should tell him for your own peace of mind. Don't feel like you have to give every little detail. That isn't important. Just let him know you've made mistakes like everyone else in this world, that you've learned from them, and that you don't feel like it should cause a problem in this relationship.

Sarah, 19

I am dating a guy who "has a past." He didn't tell me about anything until we had been dating at least four months. It was very hard for him to tell me, and very hard for me to deal with. I had only been kissed once in my life, and now he tells me he is not a virgin and was engaged before I met him. But I'm so glad he told me. You don't have to share all the details, but you can't hide it either. Respect the other person; he will respect you in turn. I respect my boyfriend for who he is now, not for what he did four years ago. I think it is right to tell the person you're dating just so he knows you're being up-front with him. I hope he will respect you for it.

Sally, 19

ThiNk AbOuT It

Have you accepted and forgiven yourself for past mistakes? Why? Can you extend that same forgiveness and acceptance to others? How important is the past in regard to who we are as people? Can you accept and love someone who has made a lot of mistakes?

A Further Word...

God has answers to your problems.

Psalm 9:9,10   Romans 8:28-39

I Have This Problem...

Proverbs 4:18-27
Proverbs 16:32
Proverbs 3:21-26
Isaiah 41:10,11

Ephesians 4:22-27
Psalm 91:1-16
Psalm 56:3,4
Philippians 2:3,4

Questions and Stories Needed

The next *Teens Talk* will be on sexual issues. Ginny welcomes any questions you might like answered or any stories you would be willing to share (if your story is used, we'll be sure to protect your identity). Write to Ginny at the address below. And thanks!

•   •   •

Seminars Available

Ginny has designed a weekend seminar on dating and relationships that involves the kids in your group. The seminar includes a lot of "teen talk." Contact Ginny at:

Box 1184
Midlothian, VA 23113